T0341899

THE
ORESTEIA

AGAMEMNON | WOMEN AT THE GRAVESIDE | ORESTES AT ATHENS

AESCHYLUS

A NEW TRANSLATION BY OLIVER TAPLIN

LIVERIGHT PUBLISHING CORPORATION

A DIVISION OF W. W. NORTON & COMPANY

Independent Publishers Since 1923

NEW YORK · LONDON

For information about permission to reproduce selections from this book,
write to Permissions, Liveright Publishing Corporation,
a division of W. W. Norton & Company, Inc., 500 Fifth Avenue, New York, NY 10110

For information about special discounts for bulk purchases, please contact
W. W. Norton Special Sales at specialsales@wwnorton.com or 800-233-4830

Manufacturing by LSC Communications Harrisonburg
Book design by Chris Welch
Production manager: Lauren Abbate

ISBN 978-1-63149-466-6

Liveright Publishing Corporation, 500 Fifth Avenue, New York, N.Y. 10110
www.wwnorton.com

W. W. Norton & Company Ltd., 15 Carlisle Street, London W1D 3BS

1 2 3 4 5 6 7 8 9 0

In gratitude to the poets I have had the good fortune to know

CONTENTS

Places Relevant to the *Oresteia*

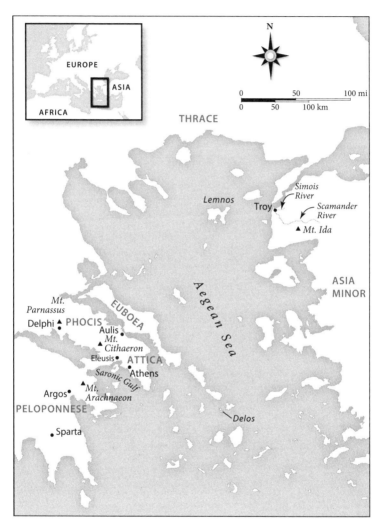

Map by Mapping Specialists, Ltd., Fitchburg, WI.

INTRODUCTION

Popular Performance

The *Oresteia* trilogy was created by Aeschylus to be performed in the open air before his fellow citizens in Athens on a spring day in 458 B.C.E. Although it comes from so early in the record of world literature, it retains an extraordinary power to grip and to provoke to this day. In fact, it is probably more widely known and widely performed now than at any other time in the last twenty-two hundred years. It remains a challenging yet accessible work which embodies conflicts about family, gender, and justice in ways that still arouse disturbing thoughts and strong emotions.

The *Oresteia* was not—and is not—just a text: Aeschylus was the director, composer, and choreographer as well as the playwright and poet. The text in this volume is the verbal record, the libretto, of a work of art that interwove action, costume, objects, dance, music, poetry, and voice. Furthermore, it did not come into being for an exclusive or elite public—and there is no good reason why it should be regarded like that today, either. It was produced, on the contrary, for an audience of at least six thousand, quite possibly many more, gathered in the *theatron,* the "viewing place" dedicated to honor the god Dionysus, beneath the walls of the Athenian Acropolis. It was a huge event, the popular entertainment of its time.

This is all a far cry from most modern theatrical experiences, which are constrained within enclosed, darkened spaces where actors move naturalistically and speak colloquial prose. Also, as well as the actors, there was the chorus, which provided an essential layer in Greek drama. Many modern productions have found that, far from being a problem, this group of witnesses, with their searching attempts to make some sense of the tragedy through their poetry and music, supply an extra, vivid dimension. This is especially true of Aeschylus' plays, where the choral songs (or "odes") are so strong and full. It makes sense that Richard Wagner, with his ideas of a "total artwork" (*Gesamtkunstwerk*), said that his impressions of the *Oresteia* molded his ideas "about the whole significance of the drama and of theater."

More recently, many of the leading stage directors have seized the opportunity to put on *Agamemnon* or the whole trilogy in order to push the boundaries of routine theater. A roll call of names gives some idea of their variety: Max Reinhardt, Jean-Louis Barrault, Tyrone Guthrie, Vittorio Gassman, Karolos Koun, Peter Stein, Peter Hall, Ariane Mnouchkine, Katie Mitchell, Michael Thalheimer. These productions have not been acts of antiquarian piety to make passive audiences feel complacent; they have been innovative explorations to provoke those who want to have their ears and eyes and emotions freshly opened.

So where did this story of theatrical revolution begin? Aeschylus was born in about 525 B.C.E., and the *Oresteia*, put on in 458, just two years before his death, was recognized as his masterpiece. The art form of tragedy had developed with amazing rapidity, given that theater, in the core sense of the word, had most probably been invented within Aeschylus' lifetime. For theater to happen, there had to be a fixed viewing place (*theatron*) and a fixed time for the audience to gather; and rehearsed players, both actors and chorus, had to be organized to enact a structured story. The evidence all suggests (though not beyond dispute) that these conditions coalesced not long before 500 B.C.E. It can hardly be coincidence that at just that same time, in 508, the Athenians radically changed their political constitution to transfer ultimate power to the people (*demos*)—in other words, they inaugurated the world's first democracy. So the first performance of the *Oresteia* may well mark the fiftieth birthday both of democracy and of theater.

The Athenian *theatron* was inherently democratic, in that it was not select or exclusive: every citizen was admitted, and the seating was not segregated or privileged. Furthermore, tragedy calls for understanding and sympathetic fellow feeling toward the situations and sufferings of other, very different people; and a thoroughgoing democracy arguably calls for an enhanced sense of the variousness of humanity and of human suffering. Open-mindedness and a plurality of viewpoints are needed if true participation in any society is to become extended to all its citizens. This is epitomized in the third play of the *Oresteia*, where the vendetta vengeance of the old aristocratic society, structured around family bonds, as seen in the first two plays, is superseded by the jury made up of citizens. This civic institution hands adjudication over to society as a whole, subsuming all other affiliations.

The theater was open, then, to all citizens. But did that extend to women, who were citizens in only limited ways that did not include participation in political decision-making or legal proceedings? Scholars are divided on this question of whether there were women present in the audience or not—there seems to be good evidence both for and against. But if they were admitted, they were still very probably a marginal minority. In that case, it is fascinating that women are so central to so many ancient

Greek tragedies, not least the *Oresteia*, where Clytemnestra and Cassandra are in many ways more powerful and intelligent figures that any of the male characters. Outside of the theater, women were restricted and suppressed, but inside that contained space the plays opened up a different perspective: the realization of their potential, their strengths and their articulacy. Clytemnestra and her tragic sisters may be portrayed as deviant and dangerous, and they ultimately come to grief, but the idea that women are far more *interesting* than society officially recognized is planted. This is central to the enduring appeal of the *Oresteia* and many other Greek tragedies.

The Three Plays

Every year three playwrights each put on three tragedies at the dramatic festival. These were normally separate plays, but in the early days connected trilogies were more common, and the *Oresteia* seems to have been the culminating exemplar of that kind of dramatic construction. The three constituent plays have been traditionally given the titles *Agamemnon, Choephoroi (Libation Bearers)*, and *Eumenides (Kindly Ones)*. These may well not go back to Aeschylus, and they are rather deterrent, suggesting to modern readers and audiences that they need to have some esoteric knowledge of ancient Greek terms before they can embark on engaging with the plays. This is not at all the case, and that is why in this translation they have been retitled as *Agamemnon, Women at the Graveside*, and *Orestes at Athens*. The argument for these coinages is set out in more detail on pp. xxx–xxxi below.

A connected trilogy would offer the obvious opportunity to tell of three generations, especially if—as so often in myth!—it was a dynasty mired in a chain of vengeance. But, instead of doing that, Aeschylus dramatizes two generations of the royal house of Argos, and then in the third play turns to an external civic context to reach for some sort of way out of the vicious cycle of vendetta. The setting breaks away from the claustrophobic family house and brings in the social dimensions of the law and politics and, by association, democracy.

Agamemnon tells how the mighty king Agamemnon comes home triumphant from the ten-year siege of Troy, undertaken to recover Helen, who had been seduced by the Trojan prince Paris. He returns, though, only to be humiliated and slaughtered by his waiting wife, Clytemnestra. He has killed his daughter and sent many soldiers to their deaths, all for the sake of recovering the promiscuous wife who cuckolded Menelaus. Clytemnestra punishes him for that, but also because she wants her own power over her own life.

The second play, *Women at the Graveside,* has Agamemnon's son, Orestes, now a young man, return from his upbringing abroad to kill his mother along with her usurping lover, Aegisthus. He kills them to avenge his father and to reclaim his heritage; but to achieve that he has to plunge his sword into the maternal breast where he once suckled as a baby. The following scene, where Orestes stands over the two dead bodies, clearly and ominously replicates that in the first play where Clytemnestra stood over the slaughtered Agamemnon and his captive Trojan sex slave Cassandra.

The *Oresteia* draws, like nearly all ancient Greek tragedies, on the inherited treasury of stories and legends about the great dynasties of a long-past "heroic" age. While these myths were fixed in some outlines, it was crucial that they were not canonical, but were open to invention and variation in detail. The common assertion that the plots were all known to the audiences in advance is simply false—the "fixed-story fallacy," so to speak. Both of the bloody episodes of the first two plays were, indeed, old stories, already familiar in Homer's epic *Odyssey* (a good two hundred years earlier), but Aeschylus has made a cru-

cial change from all earlier versions. By having Clytemnestra
single-handedly kill her husband, without the help of Aegisthus,
and by making Orestes' revenge on her central rather than that
against Aegisthus, he creates the first great female role in the
history of theater.

While the first two plays are set on the crucial days of dynastic
murder at Argos, it is part of the skillful complexity of Aeschylus' storytelling that *Agamemnon*—by far the longest of the three
plays—vividly evokes and incorporates other times and places.
Furthest back in time, the internecine conflict of the previous
generation is reconstructed. Atreus, father of Agamemnon and
Menelaus, was challenged for the throne of Argos by his brother
Thyestes, who had also seduced Atreus' wife, Aerope. In revenge,
Atreus butchered Thyestes' children, except for the baby Aegisthus, and served them cooked to their father at a feast. This
macabre tale is evoked in hallucinatory visions by Cassandra.

Another crucial "backstory," that of Helen and her elopement
with Paris, is primarily supplied by the chorus of old men in
Agamemnon. Too old to go to Troy, they still have vigorous memo-
ries. In their second great song they dwell on both the entrancing
appeal of Helen and on her dangerousness. Her delicate beauty
grows into a curse that will destroy many soldiers and the whole
city of Troy—she turns their wedding songs into laments.

But the fullest and most vivid reenvisioning of a past event
is the sacrifice of Iphigeneia at Aulis ten years earlier, recalled
by the chorus in their very first song. When the expedition was
ready to set off for Troy, the fleet was held up from crossing the
Aegean Sea by adverse winds. Following prophetic advice that
this was the only way to solve the problem, Agamemnon cut
the throat of his own daughter Iphigeneia. Not a good start—a
start that leaves Iphigeneia's mother, at home in Argos, brooding on revenge.

After all this, the third play, *Orestes at Athens*, is quite different: no blood is shed, and the drive to revenge is restrained by the establishment of a court of law. Before she was killed, Clytemnestra warned Orestes of the curse of "a mother's rabid hunting dogs." These materialize in the form of a whole chorus pack of Erinyes, ghoulish old goddesses who relentlessly pursue for revenge (on the Erinyes, conventionally known as "Furies," see p. xxx). They arrive eventually in Athena's city of Athens, and she sets up a trial for Orestes before human jurors under oath to deliver honest judgment. The votes turn out equally divided between mother and son, and Orestes is acquitted only with Athena's casting vote. In the final scene of the trilogy, she manages to restrain the Erinyes from poisoning Athens as a further transferred stage of revenge: they are to be housed and honored there, and in return to give the city peace and prosperity. This benefit is, however, conditional on the citizens' learning to respect them: the threat of the Erinyes is contained, but not extinguished.

Motivation and Judgment

The *Oresteia* is political through and through, in the sense that it multifariously explores the relationship between individuals and families within the city (*polis* in Greek) and within human society as a whole. Yet it is far from a sermon or a morality tale. It is essential that the theatrical and aesthetic experience be fully realized in its own right. Aeschylus had devoted his energies to developing the new art form of tragedy, and an awareness of the relationship between life and art is built into the work itself. The whole trilogy is thus pervaded with language and ideas about ugliness and beauty, discord and harmony, shapelessness and form, randomness and pattern. Among these, the themes of music and song recur most insistently, stretching all the way from the Watchman at the very start, who is unable to summon the comfort of song, to the call for communal music making in the closing lines of the final play. This motif enlists the poetry and visual presentation, combined with the dance and song, to draw attention to the potential place of art in human life. What is the point, the work itself asks, of crafting words and movements and sounds into a highly skilled and rehearsed presentation like this? Aeschylus, the first great tragedian, is already asking: *Why tragedy?*

There have been—and are—many answers to that question of "Why tragedy?" But a central one must be that tragedy faces full-on the fact that we humans suffer, and explores whether any understanding of this suffering is to be found: can any sense or vision can be salvaged from it? This central concern inevitably raises issues of guilt and innocence, blame and responsibility. The notion has become widespread that in Greek tragedy everything and everyone is somehow *fated,* doomed; that human creatures have no power over their destinies, and that they simply carry out what has been determined for them by some overruling force. This is in most ways a false, or at best misleading, perspective—"the fate fallacy," we might call it. While it is true that there are powers at work which are beyond the human—gods, oracles, curses, even cosmic checks and balances—Greek tragedies hardly ever show humans as in any way taken over or controlled from outside, or behaving as puppets or proxies. On the contrary, they struggle with their decisions, dilemmas, and justifications.

Clytemnestra is a striking example of this concern with the motivation and explanation of human behavior. While she does recognize belatedly in *Agamemnon* that her actions have coincided with what the family curse (the "Daimon") also determines, she proudly proclaims her deeds as her own. Her driving motives are revenge for her daughter, love for Aegisthus, resentment of Agamemnon's presumption and sexual infidelity, and protest at being treated as a subservient woman. She acts as she does precisely to show that she has the power to do so. The family curse concurs, but it does not make her do it.

Similarly, Orestes in *Women at the Graveside* has been told by Apollo's oracle that, under pain of horrific threats, he must kill his own mother. Yet, as he himself explains, he would do it anyway: he wants to be true to his father, to reclaim his ancestral wealth, and to liberate the Argive people. His motives are political and economic and impelled by family honor. He is then fully determined on the killing until the moment when Clytemnestra appeals to her motherhood. He has to be reminded of Apollo's instruction, and has to reassert his choice. But that is not the end of his psychic story: he still has to justify killing the woman whose womb had brought him to birth. It is not hard to see why Eugene O'Neill, in his trilogy adaptation of the *Oresteia* transplanted to 1860s New England, *Mourning Becomes Electra* (1931), explores Orestes and his sister Electra as studies in the Freudian subconscious. And Colm Tóibín's novel *House of Names* (2017) is also a study in the tortured psyches of family violence and hate-love, portraying Orestes as a cowed figure swept along by stronger personalities, particularly Electra.

It is crucial for the resilience of these questions of free will, determinism, responsibility, credit, and blame that for the Greeks, unlike for peoples of many other cultures, there was no clearly laid down doctrine of ultimate explanation or determinism. There is no holy book, no supreme leader, no final authority to be appealed to: any person's assessments are open to dispute and to persuasion. There are, instead, both a divine level of explanation through the gods' will, on the one hand, and, on the other, the human level of choice, decision, and deliberation. The two levels of accountability and motivation so deeply coexist that it is impossible to pull them apart: human and divine will are both variously at work in every action.

The Greeks were polytheist, and their many gods were by no means uniform or unanimous. There were many other kinds of divinity as well as the canonical Olympian gods—Zeus, Athena, and the rest. And in the *Oresteia*, there is a particularly important set of non-Olympian divine powers: the Erinyes ("Furies"), along with the Moirai and the power of the angry dead (for more on these see p. xxx). Yet, at the same time, tragedy fully makes room for a wide range of human volitions and drives, including rational thought, passion, inherited character, loyalty, deceitfulness, instinct, and resentment. Aeschylus draws all of these and more into the range of the possible explanations for his characters' behavior, as there emerges no firm explanation that is key to these portrayals of human causation. Nor is there any rationale of how these coexist with the superhuman powers, except that Zeus is in some transcendent—yet unfathomable—sense at the root of the way things are.

In a world where the higher powers are so inscrutable and uncertain, the sanctions of authority among humans are bound to be even more open to dispute. The tragedies are set in a world that is a fluid blend of a heroic, mythological society, derived from early epic, along with the contemporary culture and values of the fifth century B.C.E. This makes the conflicting human contexts even more difficult for the characters to assess for themselves. There is a constant tug between the various forces of inherited privilege, wealth, custom, military might, and personal authority, as well as the affiliations of family, city, and race. These are all assessed, contested, and challenged in different contexts during the course of the *Oresteia*. So, for example, the inherited wealth of the royal house is at stake in the family conflicts, yet it is not taken to be an unquestioned blessing. Great wealth can bring dangers with it and is liable to corrupt, as is seen in the story of Troy as well as in the power struggles at Argos.

Gender and Justice

The issues explored in the *Oresteia* extend beyond the individual and the family to the broader society, and even to humanity as a whole. Some of the leading ways the trilogy retains its accessible complexity—and its modernity—reside in the larger questioning of the social, political, and juridical issues that are implicated in the storytelling. This kind of complex of live issues, conveyed through plotting, betrayals, and dilemmas, can still inform powerful modern retellings. These include, for example, Theo Angelopoulos' extraordinarily evocative film *The Travelling Players* (1975), set in war-torn Greece from the 1930s to the 1950s, and Robert Icke's gripping contemporary re-creation, still called *Oresteia* (2015).

The two issues that stand out most prominently are probably those of gender and of vengeance. Women were, generally speaking, subordinated and disenfranchised in ancient Greek society; they were not empowered to participate in their own right in political and legal procedures; they were expected to keep quiet and to stay out of sight. Yet the important place they have in many tragedies stands in tension with this external hierarchy. The plays betray a fascination with women's forcefulness and intelligence and with their potential challenge to men. In the *Oresteia,* Clytemnestra stands as the prototype for the figure of the wronged woman who fights back with all her powers of expression, guile, and force. She has a mesmerizing control over language and over practical planning, as well as a strong arm and a ruthless determination to kill—and she is proud of it. This is the Clytemnestra who inspired Martha Graham's dance drama of 1958 and the assertive, openly sexual woman who dominates the first part of Seamus Heaney's compelling poem *Mycenae Lookout* (1996) with her "love-shout" that is like the yell of attacking troops.

Clytemnestra's marital involvement in the revenge chain also brings to the fore the two basic kinds of familial bond and sets them in discord: the parent-child bond of continuity through seed and blood is pitched against the conjugal bond through marriage and procreation. This antithesis is built up by Aeschylus into a full-scale conflict of gender. Again and again the personal confrontations are generalized into terms of "men" and "women," "male" and "female." These plays, made and performed by men for men, nonetheless give the female a seriousness and strength that cannot be dismissed or lightly patronized.

The gender conflict culminates in the trial scene in the third play. The issue of Orestes' liability for murder could be definitively settled if only it were agreed that one sex is less significant or less essential that the other. And this is what Apollo attempts to argue on Orestes' behalf: that the mother is not a true parent but merely an incubator for the father's seed. It is crucially important that this side of the case gains only half of the jurors' votes: half the votes go to the Erinyes and Clytemnestra. Apollo's argument from obstetrics is not, then, endorsed by the play— and it rings as even more objectionable today, of course. At the same time, its provocativeness taps into a deep and widespread anxiety about the hierarchy of blood relations, and about the split loyalties of children caught between estranged parents.

The other notably prominent sociopolitical concerns cluster around the nexus of retaliation, revenge, and justice. Arguably, the first response to pay violence back with violence is hardwired in animals, not excluding humans. And the history of the royal house at Argos exemplifies how blood that is unnaturally shed cries out for more blood. The first two plays of the trilogy show the addition of two new generations to the saga of vendetta in a way that sets up the question of whether this chain of consequence can ever be broken. In *Orestes at Athens,* the goddess Athena, in combination with her citizens, inaugurates a court to try cases of homicide in order to deliver a reasoned and concluding verdict one way or the other. The closing scene then goes on to face the further truth that a legal verdict does not make the desire for revenge simply evaporate; this persistence is conveyed through the continuing fury of the Erinyes, leading to their threat to blight the whole future of the city of Athens. What society has to do, the play suggests, is not to deny the urge to revenge but, somehow, to contain it and keep it in reserve. Yaël Farber powerfully recast the *Oresteia* to explore these very live issues in post-apartheid South Africa in her play *Molora* (2007).

The final scene of the trilogy might also be interpreted as bringing out an analogy between how vengeance is to be contained within civic bounds and how, if it is to have a beneficial effect within society, tragedy needs to be experienced and assimilated within the time and place of the theater. The terrifying Erinyes are placated by Athena: instead of being rejected, they are given an underground home and cult, incorporated into the very foundations of the city. But they are not finally disarmed or disempowered. As long as the city remains stable and its individuals live good lives, they will confer blessings; but if things go wrong, they will again exert their deadly threats. In live performance, this presents the integration of a beautiful terror into social life. Yet this containment is conditional, so that it holds in place a potential either for song or for misery, either for gracefulness or for ugliness. Tragedy itself, like the Erinyes in the end, has the potential to be at the same time both horrifying and enthralling, distressing and wonderful.

Theatricality of Action and Sound

This concern with ideas and issues should not suggest that the *Oresteia* is static and abstract—far from it. Everything is conveyed though vivid and constantly surprising theatricality—

all the more astonishing when we remember that until fifty years earlier, there was no such thing as theater: no staging, props, or costumes, no enactment. We are not in a position to reconstruct Aeschylus' original performance, of course, and there is much that we simply cannot know about how it was done, but the words and the shaping of the plays do still indicate quite a few theatrical scenes and features. These start with the Watchman on the roof at the beginning of *Agamemnon* looking out for the distant beacon fire—an anticipation of the first scene of *Hamlet!*—and they end with a spectacular torchlight procession.

There is, once we begin looking, a wealth of visual material: flaming torches, trails of blood, snake-entwined Erinyes, bodies tangled in nets. For such early theater, the *Oresteia* makes extraordinarily inventive use of costumes, portable objects, background buildings, tableaux, rapid movements, handing over, running away, and more. These supply many opportunities for modern productions to set them in their own aesthetic staging in one form or another.

Two great scenes demonstrate this theatrical inventiveness. First the "path of purple cloth." Agamemnon has returned in triumph on a wheeled carriage of some sort; but before he can step down from it, Clytemnestra has a path of precious purple-dyed cloths spread out in front of him and persuades him to tread over these. The scene sets a kind of enigma: Why is this action so ominous? It suggests that he walks a pathway of blood; he tramples on the wealth of his house; he submits to Clytemnestra's power, against his better judgment. And does he offend the gods by this questionably presumptuous act? Is it, perhaps, a kind of reenactment of his killing of Iphigeneia? Agamemnon fails to make direct contact with the earth of his own land, and is instead caught up in the beguilement of wealth, tangled in Clytemnestra's wrappings of words. This surely still stands as a fascinating, inexhaustible *coup de théâtre,* one of the greatest of all time.

Secondly, *Orestes at Athens* provides the archetypal theatrical stage trial. It is set up with a presiding judge (Athena), jurors, a defendant, a counsel for the defense (Apollo), and the strangest of prosecutors—the whole chorus of Erinyes, determined to exact punishment. While there are details that we cannot work out, the original action of the voting seems fairly clear: there are two urns, one for guilty, one for not guilty, and one by one the jurors hide their hands inside each of the urns and secretly drop their vote, probably a pebble, into one or the other. Once everyone has cast their vote, Athena tells an official to tip out the urns and count the pebbles. The votes in each are equal! All of this turns the judicial arguments and issues into thrilling theater.

When it comes to the *sound* of the plays, there is, compared with the visual, much less obvious direction arising from within the plays themselves, and we find much more disparity among modern productions. How like or unlike everyday, naturalistic speech is the delivery of the spoken parts to be? How much or how little music? Whether the chorus is small or large, do they speak, or sing, or do something in between? Conventions and fashions in the soundscapes of the theater are, in any case, less liable than the visual design to take much account of the original style and tone.

Still, we do have some idea, although limited, of how Aeschylus' own performance will have sounded, especially the partitions into the spoken sections and sung sections, and the relative style and diction of each kind of delivery. Most of the scenes of the plays' action were spoken, albeit in verse: a regular line that is actually to some degree comparable with iambic blank verse in English (as in Shakespeare). This meter was, we are told by Aristotle, "especially speakable." The mode of delivery for the alternating "lyric" parts, which are very substantial in Aeschylus, was quite different. These are set in complex and highly varied meters, and were mostly delivered by the chorus, although there are also passages of "lyric dialogue" involving actors. All of these lyric passages were sung with musical accompaniment, mostly played on a double pipe with reeds called the *aulos,* which combined one pipe as a drone with the other that made a piercing sound like that of a clarinet or a shawm. It is likely that, as a rule, the chorus sang in a collective unison and with one note to each syllable. The poetic diction of these parts of the play was much more highly wrought than the relatively plainspoken sections, even at times high-flown. Although they were elaborate, there is, however, no good reason to suppose that they were incomprehensible to their public. They were put there not to baffle the audience but to lead them toward a more intuitive response approached through poetry and music rather than through reason.

Modern drama does not, on the whole, embrace poetry and musicality—though there are exceptions, of course. But the *Oresteia* provides a powerful reminder of how far theater can depart from naturalistic realism, and yet still be dramatic, arguably even more highly dramatic in some ways. This translation does not try to water down Aeschylus' rich palette of phrases and images, but tries to bring out how we, the audience, are being challenged by poetry and music and color, and how that is all part of its enduring theatrical power. If it succeeds, this text may open up sights and sounds to astonish the open-minded reader, and to inspire potential performers.

ON THIS TRANSLATION

Musicality and Verse

Every translator has priorities, whether they are recognized or not; and the leading priorities of this version of the *Oresteia* are to bring out the vivid musicality of the expression and the theatricality of its potential performance. Indeed, every word of every translation is a choice; not a single word or phrase has to be rendered in one particular way. Even in translations that are supposed to be "literal" or "highly faithful," every word is chosen—and, in fact, the choices often tend toward the colorless, and the word order is often awkward. Those plain, pedestrian qualities are very far from the exuberant coloring and vigorous phrasing that characterize the language of Aeschylus.

Aeschylus was not by any measure a plain or modest craftsman of words. He was notorious already in the fifth century B.C.E. for being "lofty," piling up elaborate locutions, and glorying in coining word combinations. It is part of the texture of his theater that it is expressed in highly colored language, thick with metaphor and with constantly shifting turns of phrase. His lyrics are even further from everyday speech, piling up strange, vivid, sometimes almost hallucinogenic helter-skelters of imagery.

Translations of the *Oresteia* range from plodding prose to word whirligigs so weird that, as has been said of Robert Browning's version, it's fortunate that we have the Greek to puzzle out what the English is about! Every translation of a work from another time and place has to position itself at some point, or at various points, on a scale between the simple and mundane at one end and the outlandish and estranging at the other—between "domestication" and "foreignization," as these poles have become known. One extreme tends toward the danger of a comfortable familiarity that becomes banal, the other to an exoticism that can become a mere distraction. This version aspires, above all, to convey some sense of the vivid poetic color, the musicality, and the theatricality of Aeschylus' plays, while still keeping them accessible and without need of constant explanation. The aim is to bring across how the *Oresteia* is rich and strange and, at the same time, powerfully immediate.

So this translation is very much in verse, not prose. And the verse measures attempt to reflect the metrical and musical differences in the Greek. First, for the sections spoken by individual characters, which make up a bit more than half of Aeschylus' tragedies, the meter is relatively simple and regular. They are rendered here in English by an iambic beat, but with no regular line length. So, although there are many slight variations and syncopations, there is an underlying alternation of light and heavy syllables. Provided it is working well, readers should find an iambic pulse underpinning the pace of the lines, especially if they are read out loud.

The lyric sections, which were sung, mainly by the chorus, are much more complex. In the Greek they are usually divided into something like "stanzas" that come in pairs (sometimes known as "strophe" and "antistrophe"); and these are set in a wide variety of verse forms—in fact, the meter of each stanza pair was unique, calling for great musical and choreographic variety. This translation, which distinguishes these lyrics in the layout of the text by indentation, attempts to reflect this variety, although it is inevitably far less inventive than the Greek. Rhyme is used extensively as a way of holding together the metrical patterns; but rather than direct rhyme, there are more often variations of partial rhyme and what might be called "sound matches." The aim is to produce a sense of coherence and musicality, while not making this too pat or simplistic.

There is also a third kind of metrical mode, marked by lesser indentation, which is the anapaestic measure. These crop up in various contexts, delivered by the chorus or by actors, and were probably delivered in some kind of "singsong" chant. Thus, for example, the chorus of *Agamemnon,* when they first enter, chant for some sixty lines before they modulate into sung lyric.

Names, Especially Erinyes and the Play Titles

In any translation from one culture to another, there will be problems about names. Should they be transliterated, or rendered phonetically, or adapted? From ancient Greek into English, it has usually been the convention to use the Latin versions of Greek names, slightly adapted to English. And that is what has been done here (a concession, admittedly, to tame domestication). That means "Clytemnestra," not "Klytaimestra," and "Troy," not "Troia," and so forth. Since a verse translation like this one has to assume certain pronunciations of names, an indication of those adopted (often very different from the ancient Greek pronunciation) is supplied on p. 171.

An exception to this latinizing arises with the names of the major gods, where the Greek forms mostly supplanted the Latin back in the nineteenth century: so "Hera" rather than "Juno," "Hermes" instead of "Mercury," and so forth. The polytheistic

Greeks also recognized a multiplicity of gods beyond the well-known family on Olympus. Among the host of other divine powers, there are two collective groups of particular importance for the *Oresteia* that are still traditionally known by their Latin names: the "Furies" and the "Fates." In this translation they are given their original Greek names because the domesticated Latin forms do not do justice to their potent significance.

First, the Erinyes (four syllables in the plural—E-**reen**-new-ezz—whereas the singular "Erinys" has three: E-**reen**-noose). The English term "Furies" fails to convey the range of their associations. In the first two plays of the trilogy, the Erinyes are rather mysterious divinities who are thought of as having the task of pursuing grievous wrongs, moral or even cosmic, especially in response to family curses. They are imagined as ghoulish and horrifying creatures who lurk in the underworld and strike at humans in strange and unpredictable ways. In the third play, *Orestes at Athens,* however, they become terrifyingly incarnated as the chorus. This new physicality, an innovation by Aeschylus, changed the way they were perceived from then on, providing artists with snake-entwined figures—often rather beautiful—always ready to pursue and to punish.

The Moirai (singular "Moira") are a related group of indistinct goddesses who are repeatedly referred to and called upon in the *Oresteia.* The standard translation, "Fates," is again inadequate. The task of the Moirai is to see that people get what they should, especially death; to put it another way, they allocate proper proportions, shares, and lifetimes. Their actual operations are even more inexplicit than the Erinyes', but they are felt as an underlying current in the moral universe.

So the Erinyes and Moirai are here foreignized away from the familiar Furies and Fates. There is a curiously contrary situation with the titles of the plays. They have traditionally been given rather remote, esoteric forms that in this translation are changed to newly coined, more accessible replacements. The traditional titles—*Agamemnon, Choephoroi,* and *Eumenides*—were those registered in the official Athenian records, but they may well not have originated with Aeschylus. In fact, there is some reason to think they did not.

There is no problem with the first play being called *Agamemnon,* since it centers on his return from the Trojan War—although, in view of the much greater and more powerful role of his waiting wife, it might have been better called *Clytemnestra. Choephoroi,* the second title, means "people bringing libations" and is derived from the first appearance of the chorus as they bring offerings to pour upon Agamemnon's tomb. This ritual is unfamiliar to modern audiences, and the English version *Libation Bearers* has a musty, off-putting ring to it. I have taken the liberty of changing it to a more recognizable equivalent: *Women at the Graveside.*

It is the title of the third play that poses the greatest problem and has the least meaning for modern ears. *Eumenides,* which has been given varying translations but is most often rendered by the clumsy locution *The Kindly Ones,* is also related to the chorus. The term *Eumenides* became used as a kind of euphemistic cult term for the Erinyes, but this word is never actually used in Aeschylus' play, not even after their conciliation with Athena and Athens at the end. It is also misleading in that it fails to convey the threatening role of the Erinyes: while they are benevolent in the final scenes, they are still dangerous. So I seriously considered using the foreignizing title *Erinyes,* but I have ultimately turned to the central event and named the play *Orestes at Athens.* This recognizes the ordeal of Orestes and brings out Aeschylus' bold move of transporting the action from Argos to the city where the tragedies were first performed.

Text and Line Numbers

This *Oresteia* has been translated from the Greek without inter-mediary versions, and compared with some modern versions, it is relatively "close." There is, however, one passage where the order of the Greek text transmitted to us has been substantially altered, in order to place Athena's speech founding the court at Athens in *Orestes at Athens* at the beginning, rather than the end, of the trial scene (see Scene 7, with note on 'After 573'). Otherwise, there are no significant additions except for those rare places where there is good reason to think that something has dropped out from the original text (such additions are put inside angled brackets: < . . . >). The Greek text has hardly any external stage directions, and so almost all of those have been added, following inferences from the internal indications.

On the other hand, this translation is not totally and utterly complete, and it does not pretend to include every single phrase, nor even every line, that is to be found in the Greek text as trans-mitted to us. There is a fair scattering of omissions and trimmings; and while many of these cuts are brief phrases, there are also some lines and even longer stretches that are not included (the larger omissions are indicated in the endnotes on pp. 165–170).

There are three main reasons for these editorial prunings. First, the text transmitted to us includes, unfortunately, fre-quent places where the original has become seriously corrupted. While many of these passages have been edited to arrive at some intelligible meaning, there are also some where, in the interests of producing a fluent version, it has seemed preferable to pass over the problematic glitch. There is a scattering of places where the text is reasonably secure but includes some subject matter which would be obscure for most modern readers, such that additional explanation would be needed. So in some passages here and there throughout the plays, words and phrases have been pruned because the criteria of accessibility and of momentum have been given priority over the inclusion of everything in the Greek. The third reason for omissions is even more subjective. While the expression of the Greek is mostly tight, there are some places, especially in the spoken dialogue scenes, where it strikes modern ears as rather wordy or labored. So some cuts, usually of only a few words, have been made, in the interest of making the script more pacey and direct. These clippings are inevitably a matter of judgment, open to dispute. But ultimately, after all, every word of every translation is, it must be emphasized, a choice, an ordering of priorities.

The text registers line numbers according to the conventional numeration that has been almost universally employed in modern times; this is derived ultimately from early printings of the Greek text. These traditional numbers often, but by no means always, correspond with every tenth line of this translation. Even without the trimming just discussed, it is simply impossible for a fluent verse translation to remain tied to the fixed numeration. When marginal line numbers appear in parentheses, this is usually because the line with that conventional number has for some reason been omitted. Parentheses are also used to indicate the rare occasions where several lines have been transposed from the order in which they come in the manuscripts to a place where they make better sense.

In conclusion, this translation is not prosaically literal, nor is it colloquial and naturalistic. Its language is crafted to be rhythmical and expressive; at times it is idiomatic, at times exotic or with touches of the archaic, as is the poetry of Aeschylus in places. Cumulatively it aspires to flow, to stir up sights and sounds, and to move the reader toward horror and wonder intertwined with questing thoughts.

AGAMEMNON

CHARACTERS

WATCHMAN, under instructions from Clytemnestra

CLYTEMNESTRA, wife of king Agamemnon, left at home while he is away fighting at Troy

HERALD, sent home with news in advance of the victorious Agamemnon

AGAMEMNON, king of Argos, son of Atreus, joint leader with Menelaus of the expedition against Troy

CASSANDRA, beautiful daughter of Priam, king of Troy, endowed by Apollo as a prophetess, brought back as a slave by Agamemnon

AEGISTHUS, lover of Clytemnestra, son of Thyestes, who was the brother of Atreus, with a grudge against him

CHORUS, elders of the city of Argos

[PLACE: *In front of the palace at Argos, ancestral seat of* AGAMEMNON *and his brother Menelaus.*]

Scene 1

[Not yet day. The WATCHMAN *can be discerned on the roof of the palace.]*

WATCHMAN

I beg you gods: release me from this drudgery,
this year long spent as lookout,
time I've crouched through like some watchdog,
bedded up here on the palace roof of Atreus' sons.
I've got to know the gathering of the stars,
distinguishing those sparkling dynasties
which bring the winter and the summer with their rise
    and fall.
And now I'm watching for a token marked in flame,
the gleam of fire that brings a word from Troy:

10   the message it has fallen.
And in control of this there waits a heart in hope,
a woman's heart that organizes like a man.
But as I pass the night upon my restless dew-drenched bed—
it is unvisited by dreams, this bed of mine,
because it's fear, not sleep, that visits me
and stops my eyes from closing fast—
whenever I would like to sing or hum,
dispensing music as a healing antidote,
instead I weep for how this house has met bad times,
not managed for the best as once it was.

20   Now, though, let's hope there'll be
a bright release from all this pain:
the flame in darkness that declares good news.
    [Silence while he watches . . . he sees the distant beacon.]

The beacon! Welcome!
beaming through this night as bright as day!
There will be carnivals of song and dance
in Argos at this happy turn.
    [*He cries out in jubilation.*]
I'm calling clear to Agamemnon's wife:
stir out of bed, and quickly as you can
raise through the house a triumph-cry
in celebration of this flame.
The town of Troy is overthrown!
30   the beacon-message tells us clear.
I'm going myself to start a jig of joy
to match my master's winning throw,
because this beacon-watch has cast a triple six.
At least I hope to greet the ruler of this house
and clasp his much-loved hand in this of mine.
As for the rest, I'm keeping quiet—
a hulking ox is standing on my tongue.
The house itself, if it could find a voice,
would speak out all too clear.
I'm saying this to those who know my drift:
for those who don't . . . it's slipped my mind.
    [*He goes; the* CHORUS *of elders enters.*]

Choral Song

CHORUS

40   Ten long years now since the day that
          Menelaus, prosecuting
          Priam, strongly honor-bonded
          with his brother Agamemnon—
          double-rulers, Zeus-descended—

launched their thousand-ship armada
from this country, battle claimants.
"War!" they cry out, "war!" and shrieking
sail like eagles high above their
50 emptied eyrie; range in anguish
for their children; wheel in spirals,
rowing with their feathered oar-strokes,
since they've wasted all that labor,
nest-patrolling for their hatchlings.
High above some god does hear them—
Pan or Zeus or lord Apollo—
hears the piercing, keening bird-cry;
sends against the trespassers a
late-avenging Erinys.
In this spirit, Zeus, who guards the
60 rights of host and guest, dispatches
Atreus' sons against prince Paris;
all about a much-manned woman,
he imposes grueling struggles—
knees in dust and splintered lances—
pressed on both the Greeks and Trojans.
That is where these things are poised now,
heading for the end that's destined:
70 no amount of sacrificing
can placate relentless anger.

As for us, back then we had no
strength to offer with our wasted
muscles, so we stayed behind here,
propped up on these wooden crutches.
There's no camp for war within us;
and the very old, with leafage
80 dry, already withered, drift on

triple-footed journeys, shadows,
merely dreams by daylight.

What's the news, queen Clytemnestra?
what's the message that has led you
to proclaim these sacrifices?
All the altars flame with offerings
to the gods who help the city—
those of sky, earth, meeting-places—
everywhere the flames are leaping,
conjured by the purest resin,
ointments from the royal storehouse.
Tell as much as you are able
and is proper: do your best to
cure this anxious fear that plagues us.
Sometimes it recurs malignant,
while, at others, soothing hope comes
from your sacrifices, fending
off the heart-devouring anguish.

Since this god-given gift
has stayed with me strong
through my whole life, the power
of persuasive song,
I can command the art
to evoke in words
the omen that sent off
our departing lords.
So I shall tell of those
birds of prey that faced
the double chiefs of our
Greek youth on their quest
to take their vengeful spears

to Troy's distant shore—
kings of birds to match
our kings of the oar.
One eagle's tail was black
and the other's white;
they flew along the camp's
spear-hand, to the right,
and made their perch where all
could observe them clear:
they tore their talons' prey,
body of a hare—
a hare whose womb was crammed
with its embryo-young,
stopped short while racing on
120   its life's final run.
    Cry out, cry out with grief, I say;
    yet hope what's best will win the day.

The prophet Calchas saw
those who rent the hare
reflected Atreus' sons,
the contrasting pair.
He spoke this prophecy:
"Once proper time's passed by,
this invading force
130   is bound to conquer Troy—
the city sacked, and its
human animals
massacred in flocks
within their own walls.
My only fear's that some
god will take offense,
and stain the curb of Troy

tarnished in advance.
For Artemis is stirred
by compassion's pangs;
resents her father's cruel
terriers with wings,
who sacrifice the hare's
still-born leverets.
It is this eagles' feast
Artemis detests."
     Cry out, cry out with grief, I say;
     yet hope what's best will win the day.

140   "Artemis is so gentle,
favoring new-born nurslings,
fond of the suckling kittens
of every ranging creature.
So she demands atonement,
balance for this defilement.
Partly propitious I see,
partly malign, this portent.
I am disturbed in case she
should generate relentless
counterwinds, ship-detaining,
stopping the Greeks from sailing.

150   Don't, goddess, stir that other
sacrifice with no music,
no celebratory feasting—
that architect, inbred worker
of quarrels, who fears no husband.
For waiting behind is lurking
a frightening, reawakening,
devious house-caretaker,
long-memoried, child-avenging

Fury." This was what Calchas
prophesied from the bird-signs,
mixed with good for the royal
household as they departed.
Sing this refrain in chorus:
    "Cry out, cry out with grief, I say;
    yet hope what's best will win the day."

160   Zeus—
whoever he may be—but Zeus,
if he's contented with that name,
remains the title I shall use:
there is no other key or claim,
none to compare, if I should try
to balance all the world by weight,
except for "Zeus": no, not if I
still hope to cast my mind's disquiet
(167)   away in all reality.

(176)   Zeus—
who set us humans on the road
to finding wisdom on our own,
and fixed this precept for our good,
the truth that "learning comes through pain."
Through hearing its persistent drip,
180   the agony of pain recalled
molds our thoughts in place of sleep;
and brings sound mind, although not willed.
This favor from the gods' high throne
is kind but forcibly laid down.

So was it for the elder king,
commander of the great Greek fleet,

not blaming seers for anything,
but breathing as the winds inflate,
when all the host was stuck aground,
because the ships could not set sail,
and all the soldiers were worn down,
their stomachs filled with hunger's pain,
190   pinned where the surging currents roar,
encamped on Aulis' sandy shore.

The winds unrelenting
from the northeast sent them
idleness and hunger,
insecure at anchor,
constant people-chafing,
rotting ship and cable,
stretching out the days redoubled,
scouring the Greek bloom to stubble.
Then a grimmer course was offered
200   to the leaders by the prophet,
medicine for the bitter tempest.
This solution, naming
Artemis as plaintiff,
made the sons of Atreus
beat earth with their scepters;
and there was no keeping
bitter tears from dropping.

The elder king then poses
his dilemma-choices:
"Heavy chaos waiting
for my not obeying:
heavy, though, the future
chaos if I butcher

my own household's precious glory,
210 stain my hands with daughter pouring
life-blood on the altar table.
Which of these is free from evil?
How can I desert my navy?
How betray my allies?
For their keen desire cries
for the wind to fade now,
for a virgin's blood now.
All that's right forbids this:
may what's best conclude this."

Once he had placed his neck beneath the harness
of what had to be,
220 he veered the breathings of his thought to godless,
rank impiety.
From then he turned his mind to foster plans of
sheer audacity—
for clever, scheming madness, trouble-starting,
can make people bold.
And so he steeled his hand to grasp his daughter's
sacrificial blade;
did all this to support a war of vengeance
for a woman's bed.

They count as nothing all her "father"-cries, her
pleas, her virgin-years,
230 those battle-loving lords. The father tells his men
to pray and then to raise
her high above the altar like a goat-kid
for the sacrifice;
with all their will to hold her and her trailing
robes in readiness,

neck facing down. They tie a fetter round her
lovely cheeks and face,
a gag to hold her tongue from words to put her
house beneath a curse.

They used the bridle's brutal force
to muffle up her voice;
and as her saffron-tinted cloth
fell pouring to the earth,
240   she shot each leader standing by
an arrow from her eye,
imploring pity. Beauty standing out
as in a work of art,
she longed to call out all their names,
since there were many times
she'd sung the maiden paean-hymn
within her father's hall,
to chime with their third good-luck toast,
and grace her father's feast.

What happened next upon that day
I neither saw nor say.
The things that Calchas' skill foretold
did not go unfulfilled.
250   The scales of Justice weigh out gain
to those who've learned from pain:
but as for what the future bears,
you'll hear as it occurs.
Let be: it will emerge as bright
as when the dawn brings light.
Let's hope the rest at any rate
will turn out fortunate,
as we would wish, the old and loyal,
this land's defensive wall.

Scene 2

[*Enter* CLYTEMNESTRA *from the palace.*]

CHORUS LEADER

I'm here in homage to your power, queen Clytemnestra,
since it's right to show respect
toward the consort of a ruler,
260   when the throne's been emptied of the male.
I would be glad to know from you if you are sacrificing
in the knowledge of some firm good news,
or in the hope of hearing something welcome . . .
but I'll not object if you stay silent.

CLYTEMNESTRA

May dawn deliver her good news
that's born from kindly mother night.
Here is intelligence more joyful far than could be hoped for:
yes, the Greeks have taken Priam's city.

CHORUS LEADER

What do you mean? I can't quite catch your words as real.

CLYTEMNESTRA

Troy's fallen to the Greeks—do I make that clear?

CHORUS LEADER

270   I am so overwhelmed with joy I can't restrain my tears.

CLYTEMNESTRA

Your eyes profess your loyal thoughts.

CHORUS LEADER

But what are you relying on? Have you clear proof?

CLYTEMNESTRA

Of course I have, unless a god has played a trick on me.

CHORUS LEADER

Is it the tempting vision of a dream that you put faith in?

CLYTEMNESTRA

I'd not accept the mirage of a drowsing mind.

CHORUS LEADER

Then has some fluttering rumor lifted you?

CLYTEMNESTRA

You are insulting my intelligence as though I were some girl.

CHORUS LEADER

How long ago, then, was the city taken?

CLYTEMNESTRA

I told you: in the kindly night that gave birth to this day.

CHORUS LEADER

280   Tell me, what messenger could travel here so fast?

CLYTEMNESTRA

Hephaestus.

It was he who sent the bright gleam blazing on its way
from Troy's Mount Ida; and then beacon after beacon
passed along a chain of couriers to here.
The hills of Ida sent it to Hermaeon crag on Lemnos;
from that island, next the towering promontory
of Athos took in hand the mighty torch.
Then, flaring bright to leap across the sea's rough back,
<the flame-light reached Peparathos,
where piles of resin-pine passed on>
the golden sunlike messenger to make its landfall
on the lookout peak of Macistos.

290   That stage was not delayed by carelessness or sleep,
but flashed the beacon-signal far across the straits of Aulis
to the watchmen on Massapion.
They kept the sequence going strong by lighting heaps
of dried-out brushwood, so the torch undimmed
jumped right across the plain of Asopus
to rouse the next link of the chain high on Cithaeron's crags.

(300)   The watch there kindled even more, and sent the beacon

swooping over Gorgon Lake to Mount Geranion.
The men there waiting, keen to follow, sent the beard of flame
across the headland overlooking the Saronic gulf.
And then it swooped and safe arrived
on Arachnacon's height, our neighboring lookout point.
So finally it leapt upon this rooftop
310   of the sons of Atreus—this light,
direct descendant from the fire of Troy.
This is the way I organized my relay race
of beacons, carried to its end
by handing on from one stage to the next.
Such is the quality of proof I tell you of,
transmitted from my man at Troy to me.

CHORUS LEADER

I shall pray later to the gods, my lady;
but first in my astonishment I'd dearly like
to hear again these things that you have spoken of.

CLYTEMNESTRA

320   The Greeks are occupying Troy this very day.
And I imagine there's discordant shouting in the town.
Put oil and vinegar together in a jar,
they stay apart, irreconcilable, you'd say:
just so the sounds you hear from conquerors
and conquered—fates so different.
One side falls down and clutches at the bodies
of dead husbands, brothers, parents' parents,
as they mourn their dearest dead from throats enslaved.
330   Meanwhile the others, after roaming through the night,
all weary from the battle, turn to feeding,
hungry for whatever they can find—
not orderly but grasping at what chance may grant.
They occupy the captured Trojan dwellings,
and, relieved from camping in the open

with the dew and frost, they sleep like happy men
all through the kindly night, no need of guards.
Provided that they show due reverence to the gods
who hold that conquered land, and to their shrines,
340   the captors should not then become
the captured in their turn.
I fear, though, that the lust to plunder what they should not
may invade the troops as they give in to greed.
Remember they have yet to make their journey
safely back around the homeward section of the course.
But if the army can return
without offense against the gods,
the price paid by the dead might be appeased—
provided no disastrous twist of fate intrudes.
Well, that's the lesson that you hear from me,
the woman. May what's best win out,
(350)   and in a way that's clear beyond dispute.

       [CLYTEMNESTRA *goes back into the palace.*]

CHORUS LEADER

You've spoken, woman,
shrewdly as a man, one of good sense.
And now that I have heard persuasive evidence from you,
I shall prepare to offer to the gods due thanks,
since such high favor has been granted
in return for all our pains.

Choral Song

CHORUS

      Mighty Zeus along with star-lit
      Night in league, you threw your tightly
      clinging meshes over all the

topmost towers of Troy to make it
sure no adults, no young children
could escape the vast enslaving
trawl-net, all-entrapping ruin.
And to Zeus the host-protector,
who achieved this, I pay homage.
Long has he been waiting with his
bowstring drawn to shoot at Paris,
aiming so his arrow does not
fall short wasted, nor go flying
off above the constellations.

The hammer-blow of Zeus
you might well call it;
it can be traced to source
if you explore it.
Some people say the gods
will take no notice
when mortals trample things
which are so precious
they should not be touched—
but that is impious.
Disaster's sure for those
with too much daring,
and those whose puffed-up pride
is overbearing,
with houses full of goods
to overflowing.
Enough is good enough
for wise discretion:
a man with excess wealth
has no protection—
not once he's idly kicked

the altar-base
of mighty Justice into
darkest space.

His downfall is enforced
by hard Persuasion;
no remedy can cure
his infestation,
which glows with ghastly light
that can't be hidden.
390   Like counterfeited bronze,
with scuffs and hitting
he tarnishes to black;
once brought to justice,
indelibly he smears
his city's fortunes.
None of the gods will hear
his invocations,
as Justice crushes him
for those distortions.
One such corrupting man
was Trojan Paris,
who in the palace of
400   the sons of Atreus
breached hospitality
and decent life
by stealing and corrupting
his host's wife.

So Helen went, and left behind
military raging,
recruiting of battalions,
troops to man the navy.

She brought to Troy catastrophe
as her marriage dowry;
tripped lightly in there through the gates,
reckless in her daring.
The seer back in the palace sighed,
sensing the disaster:
"Alas the house for what's to come,
alas the house and master,
the empty bed, her trail of lust.
Sitting silent, broken,
he'll waste with pining, long for her
far across the ocean;
and it will seem the house is ruled
by a fading phantom.
Her husband takes no pleasure in
lovely shapes of statues,
because, without her living eyes,
Aphrodite's absent."

The visions that appear in his
melancholy dreaming,
though vivid, bring no true relief,
only futile seeming;
for if what seems a rare delight
slips out from embraces,
it never will rejoin the joys
that wingèd sleep releases.
Distress like this pervades the house:
yet the grief spreads wider.
For every man who went from Greece
ready for the fighting,
conspicuous in each one's house
there's a woman sighing.

This is a thing that touches all
with heart-piercing passion,
since each of those that they sent off
was a living person.
Contrast the shape that comes back home,
entering their houses,
voiceless and cold: a hollow urn
filled with crumbling ashes.

Ares makes exchange for gold,
holding up his weighing-scales
on the bloody battlefield,
trading bodies for his sales.
He refines men through his fires
into gold-dust by the ton
sent back home from Trojan pyres,
bringing loved ones heavy pain.
Ares trades men into jars,
ashes for lament and praise:
"He," they say, "knew battle skill";
"this one sacrificed his life";
"bravely in the field he fell";
"died for . . . someone else's wife."
This they growl through gritted teeth;
and suppressed resentment burns,
aggravating spread of grief,
finding fault with Atreus' sons.
Far away from here their men—
bodies that were beautiful—
win a burial in the earth
under hard-won Trojan soil.

——

With their low, resentful voice
citizens can raise a debt
that in time works as a curse.
There is a fear stays with me yet,
something roofed beneath the night:
gods maintain a watchful eye
on those who go beyond what's right,
and who kill excessively.
And the dark Erinyes
wear away relentlessly
men who have unjust success,
and they punish them below.
Those who preen with too much praise
catch the lightning bolt from Zeus.
I would choose an easy life
free from envy's ranging eye;
I'm not one to relish pain,
or to rage destructively.
May I not lay cities low,
putting people to the sword;
nor ever know captivity
subjected to an alien lord.

Prompted by the beacons, news
spread like wildfire through the city:
yet is it really true—who knows?—
or divine duplicity?
Who's so childish, wonderstruck,
as to have their heart set blazing
by some new fire-message trick,
just as liable to changes?
This kind of guesswork will occur

when control rests with a woman:
she celebrates before it's clear.
Gullible and rash, that's women;
their chattering is quick to spread,
but, once flared, is quick to fade.

Scene 3

CHORUS LEADER

We soon shall know for sure about the lookout posts
490   and message-chains of flaming beacons:
whether they were true, or whether like some dream
this light of joy has made a fool of us.
I see a herald running from the shore,
an olive garland on his head;
the cloud of flying dust is evidence
this messenger will not be one without a voice
who kindles signal-fires and smoke from mountain timber.
He shall either speak out loud a stronger call
for celebration, or . . . but I recoil
from uttering the opposite of that.
I trust he will establish well
500   what has apparently seemed well.
And if there's anyone with other wishes for this land,
I hope they reap the harvest of their own misguided thoughts.
        [*The* HERALD *has arrived by now.*]

HERALD

O soil of Argos, my ancestral country,
after ten long years I have returned to you this day!
At least I have achieved this,
even though so many of my hopes lay shattered
that I had despaired of ever dying here in Argos,

and of resting in our family tomb.
So greetings, land, and greetings, sun,
and Zeus, our highest guardian—
510   and you, Apollo, now restrain your arrows aimed at us
implacably upon Scamander's banks,
and now once more be healer and protector.
I greet you, gods of gatherings, and you,
my guardian Hermes, herald-god of heralds;
and these local hero-gods, who sent us off:
I ask you all to welcome heartily
those of our men who have survived the war.
O palace of our rulers,
and you thrones and deities in front,
now, as before, receive our king,
520   so long away, with those bright eyes of yours,
because he brings illumination
through the dark to you and all in common here:
lord Agamemnon.
Welcome him right royally,
the man who has uprooted Troy by hacking
with the blade of justice-wielding Zeus.
Their soil has been completely turned,
the country's every seed eliminated.
Such is the shackle he's imposed on Troy,
this man of happy fate, the elder son of Atreus—
530   and he's coming home.
Of every man alive he is the one most worthy
to be praised, because that Paris can no longer claim
his exploits pay more than his sufferings.
He's been found guilty of both rape and robbery:
so now he's lost his takings,
harvesting the total devastation of his dynasty—
the family of Priam has incurred a double punishment.

CHORUS LEADER

Herald from the army of the Greeks, I wish you joy!

HERALD

And joy I have. I would no longer grudge the gods my death.

CHORUS LEADER

540   Has longing for your fatherland so worn you down?

HERALD

So deeply that my eyes flood now with tears of joy.

CHORUS LEADER

Stirred up by longing for the ones who needed you.

HERALD

This country yearned for those who yearned for it, you mean?

CHORUS LEADER

So much that I would grieve with gloomy sorrow.

HERALD

But what provoked this sullen state of mind?

CHORUS LEADER

I've always said that silence is the antidote to harm.

HERALD

Some people made you fearful in the rulers' absence?

CHORUS LEADER

550   So much that, as you said, to die would be a blessing.

HERALD

Well, things have been achieved; and we could say
that some, in this long stretch of years, have turned out well,
while others are more questionable.
But who except the gods can stay entirely free
from pain throughout the whole of time?
I might describe the labors and discomforts
on board ship, the narrow gangways
where we bedded down, the many deprivations
every day provided for complaint!
And then on land conditions were more loathsome still.

We had to camp out near the enemy walls,
where rainstorms pouring down and dampness
560   rising from the ground combined to keep us soaking wet,
so all our clothing was infested by the lice and leeches.
And then the winters, cold enough to kill the birds,
with winds from off the mountain snows.
And next the heat . . . the noondays when the sea
lay fast asleep in waveless torpor.
But why complain of all these things?
The pain is past, well past—so far so for the dead
that they don't need to think of getting up again.
For us, the ones left living, benefit wins out,
and gains outweigh the losses—
(570)   so good riddance to those sufferings!
It's justified to boast before this sunlight
that the fame of our achievement
shall go flying over sea and land.
And we shall offer dedications that proclaim:
"The expedition of the Greeks defeated Troy,
and fixed these trophies to adorn the walls of shrines
throughout all Greece, a glory gleaming from the past."
580   And now that you've heard this, it's surely right
you offer praises to the country and its generals.
And thanks to Zeus who brought all this to be.
There, that's my story for you.

CHORUS LEADER

I'm gladly won round by your speech—
capacity to learn stays ever youthful in old men.
But all these things, besides enriching me,
should rightly most concern the house,
and Clytemnestra.

> [As the HERALD is about to go in, CLYTEMNESTRA comes out
> through the door.]

CLYTEMNESTRA

A while ago I raised my joyful triumph-cry,
back when the fiery messenger first came at night
to tell me of the capture and the sack of Troy.
590 And there were some who carped:
"What? Put such confidence in beacon-fires
as to suppose that Troy has now been taken?
Just like a woman to allow her heart
to be so easily elated!"—
they made me sound a lunatic.
All the same I offered sacrifice,
and, following the female custom,
throughout all the city first one woman here,
and then one there struck up the triumph-cry of joy,
and in the temples made the altars smoke with incense.
So now there is no need for you to talk to me
at greater length, when I shall hear
the tale in full told by the king himself.
600 I must make efforts, though, to welcome
my respected spouse as finely as I can when he arrives.
What day is sweeter for a wife than this:
to open wide the gates before her man
when he's been safely brought home
by the gods from his campaigns?
So give this message to my husband:
to return as quickly as he can, the darling of the city.
And he should find his wife at home, as faithful
as the day he left her, guard dog of the house,
so loyal to him and fierce against his enemies.
In keeping with this task I have not broken
610 any seal or lock in all this stretch of time.
I have no deeper knowledge of enjoyment

or of scandal with another man
than I know how to dip and temper red-hot metal.
So there's my boast, brim full of truth,
appropriate calling from a noble woman.

[*Exit* CLYTEMNESTRA *back into the palace.*]

CHORUS LEADER

So that is what she says to you;
and clear enough, if taken with interpretation,
speech that may sound well and good.
But tell me, herald, what of Menelaus?
Is he, the much-loved ruler of this land,
returning safe along with you?

HERALD

620   There is no way that, if I give a false account,
it would sustain true friends for long.

CHORUS LEADER

I wish you could give news that is both good and true:
but if the two are split, there is no way to hide the rift.

HERALD

He's disappeared. The truth is that the man himself,
and his ship too, are missing from our fleet.

CHORUS LEADER

But did he set sail by himself from Troy?
Or did a tempest tear him from the rest of you?

HERALD

Like a skillful archer you have hit the mark,
and put a great disaster in few words.

CHORUS LEADER

630   And do the other sailors reckon him alive or dead?

HERALD

There's none can give a sure report,
except the Sun that nurtures all that grows on earth.

CHORUS LEADER
　　So tell us how this storm that struck the fleet began and
　　　　ended.

HERALD
　　It's not appropriate to sully a propitious day
　　with telling of bad news.
　　Suppose a messenger, his face all sorrow, has to tell a city
　　of atrocious sufferings for their defeated army,
640　　and to bring one common wound for all the people;
　　it's then appropriate for one who's burdened
　　with a task like that to chant
　　a paean-hymn for the Erinyes.
　　But when a messenger comes with good news
　　about successes to a city that's rejoicing . . .
　　how on earth am I to mix up good and bad
　　with telling of the storm
　　the gods brought down against the Greeks?
650　　Two powers that have been always enemies
　　conspired together, Fire and Sea,
　　and sealed their pact by shattering
　　the wretched navy of the Greeks.
　　During the night a hell of waves arose:
　　gales from the north collided ships together,
　　driven by the lightning-swirls and pelting torrents
　　into goring one another's flanks,
　　until they got all scattered, as though chased
　　by sheepdogs ordered by a vicious herdsman.
　　And when the shining sun arose, we saw
　　the plain of the Aegean waters blossoming
660　　with corpses of Greek men and debris of their ships.
　　But as for us, our ship survived unscathed,
　　thanks to the stealth or pleading of a god—
　　it was no human took the helm,

but our preserving fortune must have steered
to rescue us from being swamped
upon the open sea, or driven on the rocks.
Then, once we had avoided watery death,
we turned our minds by light of day toward
670   this new disaster that had smashed our fleet.
And now if any of the others still remain alive,
they must be thinking we are drowned,
just as we think the same's befallen them.
But may things turn out for the best.
And Menelaus you might think, if anyone,
will get safe back, if light shines somewhere
on him still alive, thanks to the schemes of Zeus,
who does not wish his line to die out yet.
In that case there is still some hope
that he'll return back home.
680   Now that you've heard all this, you've heard the truth.

[*Exit the* HERALD.]

Choral Song

CHORUS

Who could have named her quite so fitly?
—unless it was some unseen deity,
one whose foreknowing tongue dictated
precisely what was to be fated—
matching the war-in-law bride, spelling
her proper name for conflict: Helen,
which predicts hell for ships and sailors,
and hell for soldiers, hell for cities.
690   She sailed from her fine-spun bower,
with zephyrs from the west to blow her,

pursued by many men with sword blades
behind the ripples of her oar blades,
until they reached the leafy babble
of Simois—through blood-stained Trouble.

Wrath brought to Troy a fateful marriage—
"marriage" that aptly sounds like "damage."
This god-sent Wrath drove to the finish
its sentence, after time, to punish
insults against the host-shared table
that Zeus himself protects as central;
to punish the song that rose raucous,
from her new family's wedding chorus.
But Priam's ancient town is learning
a newer kind of tune, and turning
that song to soulful dirge inside them,
renaming Paris "deadly bridegroom."
He brought a wave of devastation
that spilled the blood of his whole nation.

Once there was a man
who raised a lion cub
starved of mother's milk;
hand-fed it like a babe,
raised it in his house.
And through its kitten-time
it was a playful pet,
beloved by children, tame,
favorite for the old,
and often cradle-held,
dandled in their arms
like a human child.
It nuzzled fondly,

and with a shining eye
looked up at their hands
to be fed, hungrily.

But, as time went by,
it grew mature and showed
the inherited
true nature of its blood.
As repayment to
its rearers for their help,
it showed gratitude
730   by slaughtering their sheep;
served the household with
an uninvited meal—
many cruelly killed,
and blood splashed round the hall.
The creature that was housed
in its infancy
was god-raised as a priest
of catastrophe.

To Troy's old citadel there came
in early days, one might well say,
740   a sense of calm tranquility,
a jewel of prosperity;
her glance shot out a gentle dart,
rose of desire to pique the heart.
She brought them, though, a bitter end
by twisting round that marriage-bond.
She was for Priam's family
a bad inmate, bad company,
dispatched by host-protecting Zeus
to make brides weep, an Erinys.

—

750   There is an age-old commonplace
that when a man's wealth multiplies
and crops with gain a thousandfold,
it does not die without a child,
and from a growth so bountiful
bad trouble springs insatiable.
But I for one do not agree:
I say it is the evil deed
that later grows in quantity,
760   and copies through heredity.
The houses that keep justice straight
will breed a line that's fortunate.

And ancient arrogance
has a way of breeding
new young arrogance
in human evil dealing.
When it comes, the day,
one time or another,
that appointed day
gives birth to fresh anger.
770   Godless insolence,
too intense to master,
makes the house collapse
engulfed in dark disaster.

Justice radiates
in houses smoke has tarnished;
Justice elevates
the man whose life is honest.
Mansions decked in gold,
where grasping hands are dirtied,

she condemns as soiled,
and leaves with eyes averted;
780   wealth-power she disdains
as a mere illusion
falsified by praise.
She guides all to conclusion.

Scene 4

[AGAMEMNON *approaches on an open carriage, with*
attendants; CASSANDRA, *who has the robes and regalia of a*
prophet, sits behind him.]

CHORUS LEADER

Welcome, mighty sovereign, sacker
of the Trojans' city, son of
Atreus. What way should I greet you?
How to pay due homage, yet not
overshoot, nor send my arrow
falling short of proper honor?
There are many who have wrongly
favored seeming over being.
Just as all are prompt to grieve with
790   someone who has suffered, yet no
anguish stabs their deepest feelings:
so too people make out that they
take delight in someone else's
happy fortune, while they're forcing
mirthless faces into smiling.
There's no way, though, that a person's
look can fool the expert flock-judge,
if they merely seem to greet him
with a friendly fawning manner

which is really thin as water.
Back then at the time you led your
army off to fight for Helen—
I'll not hide it—in my eyes you
did not paint a pleasing picture;
you were steering far from wisdom's
channel when, in order to retrieve a
wayward woman, you recruited
men to face their deaths. However,
I rejoice now with deep gladness
for these labors well completed.
As time passes you'll discover
which among the city's keepers
have been honest, which corrupted.

AGAMEMNON

First it is right for me to greet this land of Argos
and its guardian gods; they share with me the credit
for this safe return, and for the justice
that I've visited upon the land of Priam.
For the gods decided on the case from listening,
not to speeches: to the death of soldiers.
And unanimously they then cast their votes
into the urn for blood, the blood of Troy and its destruction:
only hope approached the other urn, but left it empty.
And now the conquered city still remains
conspicuous by its plume of smoke;
the winds of ruination blow in lively gusts,
while dying embers spread about
a greasy stench of wealth.
For this the gods should be repaid with mindful thanks,
because we have exacted punishment
for a presumptuous act of theft.
And, in a woman's cause, the beast of Argos,

offspring from the horse's womb,
has ground the city into fragments—
I mean the armored troop, which launched its leap
at dead of night, a flesh-devouring lion
that jumped the walls and lapped its fill of princely blood.
It's for the gods that I've drawn out this prelude.

[*To the* CHORUS.]

830   Also, remembering your sentiments,
I quite agree—you have me as corroboration.
For it comes to few by nature to admire a friend
in times of happy fortune with no taint of envy.
I speak from my own knowledge:
for I can read the mirror of true attitudes,
and see that those who seemed so well disposed to me
840   were really shadows, ghosts.
And as for what remains concerning gods and city,
we'll convene assemblies that are communal,
consulting all the people, so we can consider
how to make quite sure that what works well at present
will remain effective in the longer term.
And if there's any issue stands in need of remedy,
850   we shall endeavor to avert malignant spread
by the judicial use of surgery—the knife or burning-out.
And now I'm going to go into my palace,
home and hearth, where first I shall do honor to the gods
who sent me out and now have brought me back.
I pray for Victory, as she has followed me,
to stay on steadfast at my side.

[*As he is about to descend,* CLYTEMNESTRA, *with women
attendants, comes out of the palace.*]

CLYTEMNESTRA [*to the* CHORUS]

Gentlemen, you elder citizens of Argos,
I am not ashamed to tell you of my husband-loving ways.

It's from my own direct experience
that I shall speak about the burdens of my life
860   throughout the time this man was kept at Troy.
It is a dreadful anguish for a woman
sitting by herself at home without her male,
forever listening to malicious rumors.
They would arrive, man after man,
announcing news of ever worse catastrophes.
And as for wounds: if this man here had suffered blows
as many times as was reported to this house,
he'd be more perforated than a net!
And if he'd died as often as the stories told,
he'd have to have been triple-
870   bodied, like some second Geryon.
Thanks to grim rumors of this sort,
I've had to be unbound by others from the noose
I'd fixed above and round my neck.
        [*She turns finally to* AGAMEMNON.]
And that is why our child, the token of our pledges,
yours and mine, is not here by my side,
as should have been the case: Orestes.
880   Don't be concerned at this, because a family friend
is looking after him, king Strophius of Phocis.
He wisely warned me of two grave uncertainties:
the danger you were threatened by at Troy;
and then the risk, supposing popular unrest
attempted to contrive a hostile plot . . .
there is a tendency to kick a man who's down.
So caution of this kind brings no deception with it.
And as for me . . . the wellsprings of my tears
are all dried up, with not a droplet left;
my eyes are bleared from lying late awake
890   and weeping for my beacons standing there inactive.

When I did have dreams, they were so shallow
I'd be woken by the whine of a mosquito in my ear.
And now that I've endured all this,
I can, with heart released from grief,
address this man of mine as guard dog of the fold;
the forestay that secures the ship;
the firm-fixed pillar that supports the roof on high;
(900)   dry land to storm-tossed sailors who'd lost hope;
a flowing fountain to the thirsting traveler.
I hold him worthy of descriptions such as these. . . .
But let this not attract resentment,
since we've borne so many troubles in the past.
And now, my dearest heart, step from this carriage,
but do not, great king, set down upon the soil
this foot which flattened Troy.

    [*To her servant women, who are waiting ready.*]
Come, women, get on with your task of spreading fabrics
all along the pathway he will walk.
910   Yes, let us have a passage strewn with purple,
so that Justice may escort him well
inside a home that lies beyond his hopes.

    [*The women spread out the purple cloths between the wagon
    and the door.*]
Our close attention, ever wakeful, shall ensure
that all the rest is, with the gods' help, rightly done.

AGAMEMNON

Offspring of Leda, guardian of my house,
your speech was fitting to my absence—
stretching out at length.
But proper eulogy remains a prize
it's right for others to award.
So do not pamper me in female fashion,
nor, like some barbarian, bow down to me

920   with gawping salutations.
And stop this spreading of my path with woven stuff
which might attract resentment—
it's the gods who should be honored in this style.
For mortals to take steps upon such ornaments of beauty
is, in my belief, a thing that's fraught with fear.
So pay me homage like a man, I say, not like a god.
There is a very different ring between the sound
of foot-mats and of fancy fabrics.
Keeping clear of dangerous thoughts
remains the greatest gift from god.
One should not call a life well blessed
until it has been lived right through in full prosperity.
If I can act entirely in this frame of mind,
930   then I may rest secure.

CLYTEMNESTRA

Well, tell me this in open honesty. . . .

AGAMEMNON

For sure I'll not betray my honest judgment.

CLYTEMNESTRA

Might some alarming turn have made you vow these to the
    gods?

AGAMEMNON

If someone with authority had authorized this deed.

CLYTEMNESTRA

And Priam? If he'd had success like yours . . . what do you
    think?

AGAMEMNON

I'm sure he would have stepped upon the precious cloths.

CLYTEMNESTRA

Then pay no heed to people's carping talk.

AGAMEMNON

Yet grumbling from the populace can be a powerful force.

CLYTEMNESTRA

The unresented man's the one with nothing to be envied.

940 AGAMEMNON

It's not a woman's place to show such relish for a fight.

CLYTEMNESTRA

Yet those who reap success may properly concede defeat.

AGAMEMNON

Does victory in this contest mean so much to you?

CLYTEMNESTRA

Agree! You're still in charge if you give way to me by choice.

AGAMEMNON

All right, if this is what you want:
here, somebody unlace my boots.

> [*One of* CLYTEMNESTRA'*s women unlaces and takes off his boots.*]

And as I tread upon these fabrics dyed with purple,
may no envious eye light on me from afar.
I have deep qualms about destroying
household properties by crushing underfoot
these precious cloths that must have cost much silver coin.
So much for that.

> [*Draws attention to* CASSANDRA.]

950 And now this stranger: offer her a kindly welcome—
god looks favorably from afar upon the man
who wields his power with gentleness.
No one puts on the yoke of slavery on purpose.
She's had to come along with me, the army's gift,
the bloom selected out of many captured spoils.
Well, now I've been subjected to your wish like this,
I'll make my way inside my house
with trampling on purple.

> [AGAMEMNON *steps onto the cloths and makes his way toward the door.*]

CLYTEMNESTRA

The sea there is—and who could drain it dry?
The sea produces many, many dye-shells,
an inexhaustible supply of welling purple,
960   worth much silver, rich for steeping fabrics.
Thank the gods we have a wealth of these, my lord—
this house does not know poverty.
I would have vowed to trample
on innumerable woven cloths,
if that had been prescribed by prophets
to ensure deliverance of this man's life.
As long as there's the root, the leafage
can grow back around the house,
and spread its shade against the fierce dog days.
And now that you've returned to your domestic hearth,
your coming signals warmth in winter;
970   and in summer, when the grapes are sour,
there then is coolness through the palace,
as the complete master ranges through his home.

    [*By now* AGAMEMNON *is going in through the door.*]
Zeus, Zeus, god complete,
now see my prayers through to the end;
make sure those things that you ensure
become complete.

    [CLYTEMNESTRA *and her servants follow him inside.*]

Choral Song

CHORUS

     Why does this clinging dread
     overcast me with foreboding,
     fluttering around my heart,

as I try to read the omen?
Why this prophetic chant
with no payment, no commission?
Why can't my reason spit
980   it out, dreamlike, and dismiss it?
Time has gone aging on
since the sand jumped off the cable
hauled from the ocean bed
when it sailed for Troy, that navy.

They have returned back home,
my own eyes have been the witness,
yet all the same my heart
uninstructed sings within me
990   dirge-notes without the lyre,
dirge an Erinys composes,
dismissive of the strength
that hope offers to oppose it.
My heart is churning, whirled
with the dread of due completion:
I hope my fears prove wrong—
1000   may it never reach completion.

Insatiable desire
can fill a house too full;
corruption lives next door
and leans against the wall.
A life that's laden rich
will strike on a dark reef,
unless some dread can reach
1010   it first to keep it safe,
by throwing off the side
a share of all those goods.

The house may then survive,
not sunk by its crammed holds.

Once blood has spurted black
and soaked the ground with death,
there's none can chant it back
to life from the stained earth.
An overriding fate
holds back those who transgress—
a warning that my heart
should make clear with full voice:
it lurks in dark instead,
and murmurs in its pain,
and can't unwind the thread—
meanwhile, my mind's aflame.

1020

1030

Scene 5

[CLYTEMNESTRA *reenters.*]

CLYTEMNESTRA

You! Come along inside as well—
it's you I mean . . . Cassandra.
Zeus, far from showing anger, has delivered you
where you may share the rituals of the house,
and take your place with all the other slaves
around the altar of our household Zeus.
So step down off this carriage,
and don't act aloof—they say that even Heracles
was sold to be a slave, and had to feed on barley gruel.
So since compulsion has tipped down
the balance of your fortune, count it as a blessing
you belong to masters with ancestral wealth—
those who unexpectedly strike rich prove cruel owners,

1040

while from us you shall receive what is the proper custom.

[CASSANDRA *is unresponsive.*]

CHORUS LEADER [*to* CASSANDRA]

It's you she has been speaking to, and speaking clearly.

Now that you've been captured in a fatal net,

you should obey . . . if you are going to.

CLYTEMNESTRA

Unless she speaks some unintelligible

1050   foreign tongue and chirrups like a swallow,

I should be reaching through into her understanding.

CHORUS LEADER

Go on. She's telling you what course is best for you.

Obey, and leave your seat here in the wagon.

CLYTEMNESTRA

I don't have time to waste out here.

The animals are waiting, ready for the sacrifice

before the central altar of the palace.

[*To* CASSANDRA.]

If you wish to join in this, then don't delay.

1060   Or if you can make nothing of my words,

then wave your hands instead

with alien gestures to communicate.

CHORUS LEADER

It seems the stranger needs a good interpreter;

she is behaving like some new-caught creature.

CLYTEMNESTRA

She's crazy and delusional.

She has arrived here from a conquered city,

yet she has no notion how to wear the bridle—

not, that is, before she has been broken in,

her mouth blood-flecked with foam.

I'll not waste further words on her,

just to be disrespected in this way.

[*Exit* CLYTEMNESTRA *back indoors.*]

CHORUS LEADER
    Well, I feel pity for you, so I'll not be angry.
1070   Come, poor woman, get down from this wagon;
    yield before necessity and take on this new yoke.

Scene 6

CASSANDRA
    otototototoi popoi da.
    Apollo, Apollo!

CHORUS LEADER
    Why these strange sounds about Apollo?
    He is not the god for someone who laments.

CASSANDRA
    otototototoi popoi da.
    Apollo, Apollo!

CHORUS LEADER
    There she goes again, profanely calling on the god
    who's not appropriate for joining cries of grief.

CASSANDRA
1080   Apollo, Apollo,
    appalling, you destroyed me!
    Now for a second time
    you easily destroy me.

CHORUS LEADER
    It seems she is to prophesy her own misfortune—
    although a slave, the gift remains strong in her mind.

CASSANDRA
    Apollo, Apollo,
    appalling, you destroyed me!
    What kind of home is this?
    Where's this that you have drawn me?

CHORUS LEADER

> This is the palace of the sons of Atreus,
> if you did not know—I'm telling you the truth.

CASSANDRA

> No, a house god-hating—
> it's a house that's freighted
> with much inbred bloodshed,
> where its own are butchered.
> A human abattoir,
> a blood-bespattered floor.

CHORUS LEADER

> The stranger seems keen-scented like a hound;
> she's on the track of murders, that's for sure.

CASSANDRA

> This is what confirms me,
> what I see before me:
> these little ones bewailing
> their own cruel killing,
> and the roasted meat
> their father had to eat.

CHORUS LEADER

> We've heard about your reputation as a prophet;
> but we do not need your visions.

CASSANDRA

> *io, so hard!*
> What is this, this scheming,
> what trauma is this now?
> Utter wrong this scheming,
> here within this house,
> unbearable, incurable—
> far off from all defense.

CHORUS LEADER

I cannot understand this prophecy.
I recognized that other one—it is well known.

CASSANDRA

io, so harsh!
So this is what you're hatching?
The man who shares your bed,
your husband, as you bathe him . . .
how to tell the end?
1110   Immediate, inexorable,
hand reaches over hand.

CHORUS LEADER

I still don't see. I'm at a loss to understand
the prophecies these riddles are obscuring.

CASSANDRA

e, e, such pain, such pain!
What's this that comes in sight?
It is some Hades-net;
and she who draws it tight
is she who shares the bed,
who shares the guilt of blood.
So let the gloating crew,
bloodthirsty for this race,
strike up the triumph-cry
to mark this sacrifice.

CHORUS

What sort of Erinys is this you tell to crow
1120   above the house? Your words don't cheer me, no.
The sallow drops of blood drain out
from my pale cheeks to flood my heart,
just as a wounded man's life fades
together with his sunset rays.

CASSANDRA

a, a, it's plain, it's plain!
Keep him from the cow,
the bull: she wraps the robes
around him, then see how
she springs the trap and stabs
him with her jet-black horn.
Down in the watery pool
he falls. I tell of death
by tricks enough to fill
a deadly murder-bath.

CHORUS

1130   I am no expert judge of prophecy,
but all these things you say sound bad to me.
No human good that I can tell
has ever come from prophets' skill.
Their craft and many sayings lean
to fearful things for us to learn.

CASSA A

Oh, oh, so cruel a fate!
I mean my own ordeal;
it's for *my* death I cry,
poured in to fill the bowl.
Why have you dragged me here to misery?
For nothing but to share death's agony.

CHORUS

1140   Mad-minded, god-possessed, frenetic,
to set this music that's no music
to your own fall.
You're like the nightingale for pity
with her lament of "Itys, Itys,"
perpetual.

CASSANDRA

Oh, oh, the nightingale
with her clear-ringing songs,
the gods have fashioned her
with feather-covered wings.
She has a pleasant time, no cause to wail:
for me there waits the edge of sharpened steel.

CHORUS

1150 These sorrows, god-possessed, onrushing,
these elegies you mold with passion,
where are they from?
These darkling, piercing notes of mourning,
waymarks of your prophetic journey,
where are they from?

CASSANDRA

Oh, oh, the marriage, marriage,
joined with death by Paris!
Oh, oh, Scamander's waters,
stream of my ancestors!
Back then I grew from girlhood
by your flowing whirlpools:
1160 now, though, it seems that I shall prophesy
upon the banks where Acheron sweeps by.

CHORUS

Why are your words like this?
All too precise—
even a child could hear
and find it clear.
I feel the piercing bite
of your cruel fate;
you shake me to the core
with notes of fear.

CASSANDRA

> Oh, oh, the suffering, suffering
> of my city's crushing!
> Oh, oh, the ritual slaughter
> offered by my father!
> Those sheepflocks from our meadow
> proved no cure from death, though,
> no way to stop the city falling as it had to.
> And I shall spill to earth my hot blood too.

1170

CHORUS

> The horrors that you tell
> continue still.
> Some cruel divinity
> drums heavily,
> and turns your melody
> to threnody.
> I cannot understand
> how this will end.

CASSANDRA

> No longer shall my prophecies peer out from veils,
> all coyly like a bride upon her wedding day;
> but, springing freshly like the breezes
> from the rising dawn, they'll stir a swell
> that breaks yet greater grief upon the shore.
> No longer shall I offer hints from riddling clues.
> Bear witness I'm a bloodhound sniffing keenly
> on the scent of horrors perpetrated long ago,
> because there is a chorus never leaves this house;
> it sings in unison but not in harmony—
> its theme is not benign. It is a drunken band,
> fired up by swigging human blood,
> and yet they skulk inside, refusing to be sent away.
> What are they?

1180

1190

Family Erinyes.

They occupy the rooms, and chant their anthem
of the primal wrong, denouncing him,
the one who trampled on his brother's marriage bed.
Well? Does my arrow miss, or does it hit the mark?
Am I a cheating prophet, just a burbling
fortuneteller hawking door to door?

CHORUS LEADER

    I am amazed at you: although brought up
1200   across the seas, you have the power
    to tell what happened in an alien place
    as though you had been standing by.

CASSANDRA

    It was Apollo raised me to this role as prophetess.

CHORUS LEADER

    He was enraptured with desire, you mean, a god?

CASSANDRA

    Before now I was too ashamed to speak of this:
    he twined his limbs about mine, breathing sweetness.

CHORUS LEADER

    And did the two of you join in the act that makes a child?

CASSANDRA

    I promised that I would, but then refused.

CHORUS LEADER

    Were you imbued already with god-given powers?

CASSANDRA

1210   I was already prophesying all Troy's sufferings.

CHORUS LEADER

    How could Apollo's anger let you stay unharmed?

CASSANDRA

    Since I offended him, no one believes a word I say.

CHORUS LEADER

    To us your prophecies appear convincing.

CASSANDRA [*cries with pain*]

    Again the piercing anguish
    of foretelling true comes swirling up,
    and thrums me with discordant preludes.
    Look! See these children, like the forms in dreams,
    that sit around the house.

1220   Their hands are full of meat, a home-cooked feast;
    it's their own offal that they're holding, clear—
    such pitiable portions, innards that their father gorged upon.
    And in revenge for this, I say that there is one,
    the jackal lolling in the lion's bed, the stay-at-home,
    who's plotting how to catch the master when he comes.
    The leader of the fleet and conqueror of Troy
    has no idea of how the hateful bitch
    can use her tongue, how she can fawn and lick
    and brightly dip her ears . . . then bite.

(1230)   So daring is the female killer of the male.
    What could I call this loathsome creature?
    Viper with envenomed fangs at either end?
    Or snapping Scylla lurking in the rocks, a threat for sailors?
    A hellish mother monster set on war with her own family?
    How brazenly she whooped her cry of triumph,
    as though it was a battle turning point,
    while seeming joyful at his safe return.
    It makes no difference if I fail convincing you,

1240   because the future will be coming all the same.
    And soon you shall be standing there, and pitying me,
    and calling me the one whose prophecies
    infallibly turn out too true.

CHORUS LEADER

    I recognize Thyestes and his feast of children's meat:
    it makes me shudder when I hear it so directly put in words.
    But as for all the rest I've heard from you,
    I'm trying to interpret but I've lost the track.

CASSANDRA

With your own eyes, I say, you shall see Agamemnon dead.

CHORUS LEADER

Hush now, poor woman! Do not say such things.

CASSANDRA

There is no way of curing this prediction.

CHORUS LEADER

Not if it is to be, but may it never come about.

CASSANDRA

1250   You utter prayers: meanwhile, they're readied for the kill.

CHORUS LEADER

Who is the man who's planning this atrocity?

CASSANDRA

That shows how far you've lost the track of what I've
    prophesied . . .

CHORUS LEADER

But I can't see how he'll devise a way of doing this.

CASSANDRA

. . . although my grasp of Greek is good—too good!

CHORUS LEADER

The Delphic Oracle is Greek, yet hard to understand.

CASSANDRA [cries of pain]

The fire, how it engulfs me!
Apollo, *ai ai* me!
This is the lioness that walks upon two feet,
who makes love with the jackal
while the noble lion is well away.

1260   And she is going to kill me.
Like mixing up a potion, she has added
her reward for me stirred in the brew;
and as she whets her sword to kill the man,
she gloats that he will recompense
in blood for bringing me along with him.

What reason have I, then, to keep
this token stuff? A joke against myself,
this staff and ribbons round my neck.

> [*She throws her prophetic staff, ribbons, and trappings to the
> ground, and tramples on them.*]

To hell with you!
I pay you back like this.
And see, Apollo for himself
1270   strips off this prophet rigmarole.
He does this after gazing at me being ridiculed
in this array by even dear ones turned against me.
I have had to suffer insults,
and be called a starving pauper girl,
as though I were some begging fortuneteller;
and now the prophet-god
has done with me, his prophetess,
and brought me to this kind of deathbound end.
In place of my ancestral altar there awaits
a butcher's block still warm with blood
from previous slaughter there.
And yet . . . our deaths shall not go disregarded by the gods,
1280   because another one shall come as our avenger,
a mother-killing, father-vindicating child.
A wandering fugitive, excluded from this land,
he shall return and add the topmost row of stones
to cap these kin-catastrophes.
His father stretched out there shall draw him back.
In that case, why lament so piteously?
I have seen Troy first suffering as it did;
and next the conquerors are being dealt
their turn before the judgment of the gods:
I therefore take my place as well.
(1290)   I shall be bold to die.

> [*She turns toward the door to go in.*]

This door I greet now as the gate of Hades.
And I pray I shall receive a swift, clean blow,
so that, without convulsion,
with my blood outgushing easily in death,
I close these eyes.

CHORUS LEADER

You are a woman deep in misery,
yet also deep in insight.
But if you truly know about your death,
how can you tread so resolutely,
like a god-directed heifer to the altar-stone?

CASSANDRA

There's no escaping, strangers, none.
There's no more time.

CHORUS LEADER

1300   But time is precious at the very end.

CASSANDRA

This is the day, today. To run away would gain me nothing.

CHORUS LEADER

Well, your resolve is surely rooted in a heart of courage.

CASSANDRA

No happy person ever has to hear such words.

CHORUS LEADER

It is some blessing, though, to perish gloriously.

CASSANDRA

O father, how I feel for you and for your noble sons!
    [*She advances to the door, but recoils.*]

CHORUS LEADER

What is the matter? Why recoil in fear?
Why retch like that? Is this revulsion in your mind?

CASSANDRA

The whole house reeks of murder, dripping blood.

CHORUS LEADER

1310   No, no! That's just the smell of ritual sacrifice.

CASSANDRA

It's like the fetid stench exuding from a tomb.

CHORUS LEADER

It can't be the exotic incense that you mean!

CASSANDRA [*again resolves to go*]

No longer shall I flutter like a frightened bird:

Now I shall go inside and sing laments

for Agamemnon and myself.

Enough of life.

Strangers, I ask you this: bear witness

after I am dead that I was right,

once that it's happened: that a woman

has met death to make amends for me, a woman,

and a man has been laid low

to match a badly mated man.

1320 As a stranger on the point of death,

I ask this favor of you.

CHORUS LEADER

Poor woman, I feel pity for the fate you have foretold.

CASSANDRA

I wish to add just one more word—

a swan song for myself.

I call on this, my final shining sun:

make sure my killers pay back dear

with their own blood for me,

the victim slave, the easy catch.

This is the way it is for humans:

if they have good fortune, it is like a shadow;

if they are unfortunate,

it takes a dampened sponge

to wipe the picture clean away.

1330 And I feel far more pity for these things than those.

[*Exit* CASSANDRA *into the palace.*]

Choral Chant

CHORUS

It is only human nature
never to know satisfaction
with success. And no one tries to
stop it moving into mansions
which set envious fingers pointing;
no one orders "No Admission."
This is true of *this* man even,
one the gods have favored with the
prize of taking Priam's city,
and of coming home in honor.
All the same, if now he has to
pay for murder done by former
generations, and to die for
his own killings; and by dying
1340   bring about yet further killings . . .
if all this, then who could claim that
any human may be born to
happy fortune, safe from troubles?

Scene 7

[*A cry of agony is heard from inside.*]

AGAMEMNON

Aah! I have been struck . . . deep . . . fatal. . . .

CHORUS LEADER

Keep quiet. Who is it shouting about deadly wounds?

AGAMEMNON

   Again . . . I'm struck again . . . aah!

CHORUS LEADER

   It is the king. His cries sound like the deed is done.
   We should decide together on the safest course.

CHORUS MEMBER 1

   I tell you my advice: it is to summon citizens
   to come here to the palace bringing help.

CHORUS MEMBER 2

1350   I think that we should break inside at once:
   investigate it while the sword still drips with blood.

CHORUS MEMBER 3

   I share in that opinion. My vote's for action:
   this is not the moment for delay.

CHORUS MEMBER 4

   It's clear to see: this is the overture
   to setting up a new tyrannical regime.

CHORUS MEMBER 5

   Yes! And we're wasting time, while they despise
   our caution and are pressing on with action.

CHORUS MEMBER 6

   I'm unsure what response to recommend:
   someone who means to act must plan ahead.

CHORUS MEMBER 7

1360   I go along with that. It's not as though we can
   stand up the dead again, for all our fighting talk.

CHORUS MEMBER 8

   So are we going to give in to these violators
   of the royal house, just to save our skins?

CHORUS MEMBER 9

   Intolerable! It's better to be dead—
   less bitter than to live on under tyranny.

CHORUS MEMBER 10

So do we speculate the man is murdered
merely on the evidence of hearing shouts?

CHORUS MEMBER 11

We ought to be discussing what we know for sure.
Mere guesswork's not like certain knowledge.

CHORUS LEADER

1370   I feel we are agreed: we must
find out for sure how Agamemnon fares.

Scene 8

[*The doors open to reveal* CLYTEMNESTRA *with sword in
hand, standing over the bodies of* AGAMEMNON *and*
CASSANDRA *lying, caught up in a net, in a bathtub.*]

CLYTEMNESTRA

I offer no apology for saying things that contradict
what I have said before to suit the moment.
How else, if you are planning harm
against your enemies, who think they're friends—
how else are you to rig the trap of nets
too high to be escaped by leaping over them?
My mind has long been working out
this final contest in my long-drawn feud—
and now, at last, it has arrived.

1380   I stand here where I struck,
with what I did in front of me.
I managed it—and I am proud of this—
in such a way that he could not
escape his fate, nor fend it off.
I cast around him an impenetrable mesh,
like one for netting fish, a fatal luxury of fabric.
Then I struck him twice,

and with two cries his limbs went limp;
once he was down, I followed with a third,
an offering made in gratitude to Hades,
the saver of the dead below.
And so he gasped his life away,
and spouted out a jet of blood
1390   that showered me with a drizzle of dark dew.
And I was glad, as glad as is the crop of corn
to feel the gleaming moisture, gift of Zeus,
when grain is brought to birth from out the husk.
It is a proper offering to pour
upon this corpse, this blood.
It's just, and even more than just,
because this man has filled a cup
of such accursèd crimes within this house—
and now he has returned and drained it to the dregs.
(1393)   So that is how things are, you Argive elders.
Be glad, if you are gladdened:
as for me, I revel in all this.

CHORUS LEADER

I am astounded at your brazen tongue—
1400   your bragging like this over your own husband.

CLYTEMNESTRA

You patronize me like some little woman
with no mind to call her own.
I speak with heart devoid of fear
to those with wit to understand,
and you can praise me or condemn me
as you like, it's all the same to me.
This man is Agamemnon,
yes, my spouse, and yes, a corpse,
the work of this right hand of mine,
this architect of justice.
And that is that.

CHORUS

> Woman, what detested
> earth-grown venom have you tasted,
> or drunk down what poison
> dredged up from the deeps of ocean,
> to have done this murder?
> With the people's curses shouted,
> you shall be deprived of country,
> banished with the city's hatred.

1410

CLYTEMNESTRA

Today you sentence me to exile from my country,
and to hatred from the people and their curses.
Yet back then you raised no voice against this man,
this man who rated her as nothing,
back on that day he cut his own child's throat—
as though it were the slaughter of an animal,
one from his many fleecy flocks of sheep—
the treasure of my labor pains,
used as a charm to quell the gusts from Thrace.
So isn't he the one you should have driven
from this country in atonement for pollution?
Yet when you scrutinize my handiwork,
oh, then you are the righteous judge!
I tell you this in answer to such threats:
I'm ready to submit if I am overcome
in contest hand-to-hand:
but if the god ordains the opposite, then you may learn
in your old age to think more carefully.

1420

CHORUS

> You are proud and devious,
> and the words you speak ambitious,
> just as you are maddened

in your mind, which murder's reddened.
And the blood-flecks flaring
show up on your eye-whites clearly.
You shall pay dear, friendless,
1430   trading blow for blow relentless.

CLYTEMNESTRA

Hear this, my solemn oath,
by Justice, now completed for my child,
by Curse and Erinys, the powers
I've sacrificed this man to satisfy:
no pang of fear stalks through my house,
no, not so long as one maintains
the flame upon my hearth, Aegisthus,
not while he stays loyal to me,
the shield who keeps me confident.
Here this one lies, the violator of this woman here,
the charmer of the golden girls at Troy.
1440   And here she is, the prisoner, the prophetess—
his double-bedmate, fortuneteller,
believable between the sheets—
who used to shuttle back and forth
across the benches on board ship.
And so they both have met their due deserts:
he's here like this, while she, swanlike,
has sung her final funeral dirge.
And with her lying here on top of him,
she has served up for me an extra sauce
to top my luscious feast.

CHORUS

I wish it would come quick,
not after lying sick,

nor after pain-filled years:
1450　　that final fate that draws
the never-ending dark
of sleep that does not wake—
now that our noblest guard
is lying here, struck dead.
He suffered many ways,
all in a woman's cause;
and through a woman's deed
his life has been destroyed.
Frenzied Helen, you alone
have destroyed in front of Troy
lives so many, all too many.
Now you've bound a final crown,
1460　　stained with blood too strong to scour,
you the war-cause in this house.

CLYTEMNESTRA

Don't allow these things to crush you
so you wish for death to take you.
And don't turn your anger onto
Helen, calling her the fatal
man-destroyer. It's not right to
claim that she, one woman, ended
all those lives of Greeks, inflicting
all this pain that stays unhealed.

CHORUS

O Daimon of the house,
you swoop down on this place,
and on the differing pair,
the sons of Atreus here.
1470　　And you have lavished power
upon the female pair,
so similar at heart.
It bites me deep, this hurt.

Above the body now,
like some detested crow,
it struts and gloating sings
its tuneless triumph-songs.

CLYTEMNESTRA

Now you've hit a truer version
when you name the family Daimon,
fattened for three generations.
That's what nourishes the lust for
lapping blood-pools; then, before the
ancient trauma can be mended,
1480   yet more suppuration gathers.

CHORUS

Yes, it's fraught with fury,
that strong Daimon,
never sated fully
with misfortune.
Everything that happens
comes through Zeus all-
causing, all-enacting.
What's concluded
for us humans without
Zeus behind it?
    How am I to weep for you,
1490   O my king, my king?
    What heartfelt words of loyal lament
    can I turn to song?
    You lie where you breathed your last,
    in this spider's web,
    prisoner of slavish bonds
    on this squalid bed.
    Hobbled by this deadly trick,

you met with your end,
chopped down by a two-edged blade
gripped in your wife's hand.

CLYTEMNESTRA

Are you claiming that this slaughter
is my doing? Stop regarding
me as Agamemnon's spouse, then:
no, the ancient, acrid Vengeance-
1500   spirit has assumed the shape of
this cadaver's wife. Aroused by
Atreus, heartless banquet-server,
it has claimed this full-grown victim,
further payment for the children.

CHORUS

To claim that you are guiltless
of this slaughter:
no one could stand as witness
for that falsehood.
How? How? But that some specter
might have paired you,
avenging ghost ancestral,
as a partner . . .
that is possible. And Ares,
gore-stained and dark,
will make more bloodstream channels
1510   come flooding back
to where he can claim justice
for the babies
whose flesh and clotted blood were
served at table.
    How am I to weep for you,
    O my king, my king?

What heartfelt words of loyal lament
can I turn to song?
You lie where you breathed your last,
in this spider's web,
prisoner of slavish bonds
on this squalid bed.
Hobbled by this deadly trick,
you met with your end,
chopped down by a two-edged blade
1520   gripped in your wife's hand.

CLYTEMNESTRA

In my judgment, this man's death was
no more squalid than was fitting.
It is right that he has perished
through deception, since he ruined
this whole family with deception.
Yes, the darling that I bore him,
dearly-wept Iphigeneia,
he, her father, made his victim.
Now he's suffered suitably to
match his actions. He will have no
cause to bluster down in Hades,
now he's paid by fatal sword-stroke.

CHORUS

1530   I remain at a loss,
helpless without resource
which way to turn my mind
before the falling house.
I fear the drumming storm
beating upon the home,
the deluge turned to blood,

a pelting hurricane.
Now fate whets action's edge
keen on the sharpening-stone,
preparing to ensure
that there's more justice done.
O earth, O earth, I wish you'd covered me
before I'd set my eyes
1540   on this man brought to such a lowly bed,
this bath with silver sides.
Who comes to bury him, who to lament?
Could you now have the gall,
when you have killed your man, to stand up there
and lead the funeral wail?
to favor his past life disfavoredly
in tribute for his deeds?
Who shall proclaim the graveside eulogy
1550   with heart that truly bleeds?

CLYTEMNESTRA

It is not your proper place to
raise this matter. By my hand he
dropped down, downed in death, and by my
hand he shall be laid down under,
not with mourning from outsiders.
Aptly shall his daughter greet him,
his adored Iphigeneia,
meet her father at the ferry–
landing by the aching river,
and embrace him, planting kisses.

CHORUS

1560   Damnation meets with condemnation back:
to judge is difficult.
The plunderer gets plundered in his turn,

the killer pays for guilt.
Yet this remains as long as Zeus remains
upon his throne secure:
who does the deed must suffer for the deed—
that's the eternal law.
Who can eliminate the seed, expel
the household curse at last?
This family and dire catastrophe
are glued together fast.

CLYTEMNESTRA

Yes, you've hit upon the truth with
that pronouncement. So I'm willing
1570   to agree a solemn promise
with the Daimon of this bloodline:
that if only it will go and
leave this palace, and oppress some
other house with kindred murders,
I shall be content to manage
with a fraction of our riches,
just enough and nothing further.
This I promise, if I can then
purge this household from the madness
of our killing one another.

Scene 9

[AEGISTHUS, *accompanied by bodyguards, enters abruptly.*]

AEGISTHUS

I greet you, welcome light of day that brings me justice.
I can say at last that gods look down from high
upon the crimes of earth and make sure humans
1580   pay the price, since now I see this man here

lying in the woven cloths of the Erinyes,
and paying for the plot his father perpetrated.
That father, Atreus, was the ruler of this land:
when he was challenged for the kingship
by Thyestes, my own father and his brother,
Atreus drove him out, an exile from his house and land.
Unfortunate Thyestes then returned,
a suppliant at the hearth, which was a way
to save his blood from staining his ancestral soil.

1590   But as an act of hospitality, and with enthusiasm
more than love toward my father, godless Atreus
made out to be arranging a great celebration-feast;
and there he served him up a dish of children-flesh.
He hacked away their heads and hands and feet,
and served Thyestes, as he sat apart,
with portions that could not be recognized.
So in his ignorance he ate—a dish which, as you see,
has proved disastrous for the dynasty.
Then, once he'd realized his monstrous act,
he cried out in revulsion and, recoiling,

(1600) spewed the gobbets out.
He kicked the feasting table over,
and so made it fit the justice of his curse:
"Like this I pray the whole bloodline be overturned."
In consequence of that you see this man brought low;
and I have pieced this death together with the thread of justice.
For I was the third child, left alive and driven
into exile as a little baby with my wretched father.
Justice has returned me here, now that I am full-grown;
and I have got this man into my grip,
although I was outside the house itself,
by linking the whole scheme behind this deadly plot.

1610   So even death would seem acceptable for me,

now that I've seen him tangled
in the cords of Justice.

CHORUS LEADER

Aegisthus, I have no respect for one
who acts all high and mighty in bad circumstances.
You claim you meant to kill this man,
and planned this pitiable murder:
well, I proclaim that, once you're brought to justice,
you shall not escape the people's
stones and curses flung at you.

AEGISTHUS

You dare to talk like this, although you're down
upon the lowest rowing-bench,
while those in charge are on the bridge?
1620   You'll find, when brought to see some sense,
that learning can be tough for people of your age.
Prison and starvation-pangs remain
outstanding teachers, even for the agèd mind.
You have your sight, yet don't see that?
Don't kick against the goad,
for fear you get jabbed back.

CHORUS LEADER

You stayed at home, effeminate, and schemed
against the soldier fresh back from the field;
and all the while you sullied his own marriage bed,
and planned his death, our general.

AEGISTHUS

You'll suffer long and hard for saying that.
Your talk sounds just the opposite of Orpheus:
1630   his voice was so delightful he would draw all nature to him,
while you, thanks to your howling foolishness,
will find yourselves dragged off in chains!
Once you're subdued, you'll prove a bit more tame.

CHORUS LEADER

You think that you'll be sovereign over Argos?
You, who when you'd planned his killing,
didn't even dare to strike the blow?

AEGISTHUS

Because the trickery was obviously the woman's role;
my longtime enmity made me the object of suspicion.
Yet I'll undertake to rule the people here
by making use of this man's treasury;
and anyone who's not obedient
I'll clamp beneath a heavy yoke.

1640   He'll prove no frisky grain-fed colt:
starvation rations and a pitch-dark cell
will see him turn more docile.

CHORUS LEADER

But why not strike this warrior down yourself,
you coward? Why do it through a woman,
bringing down pollution on the country and its gods?
I only hope Orestes is alive somewhere,
so he may yet return here with good fortune
to become the champion, killer of the pair of you.

AEGISTHUS

Since you've decided on this way to act with bluster,
you'll soon have to learn your lesson.

CHORUS LEADER

1650   Come on now, my fellow fighters—close to time for action.

AEGISTHUS

Come on now, my soldiers, hands on sword hilts ready.
        [*The guards grip their swords, and the* CHORUS *raise their
        wooden staves.*]

CHORUS LEADER

And my hand is ready also; and I'm quite prepared to die
here.

AEGISTHUS

Yes, your saying "die" is welcome: we accept that offer!

CLYTEMNESTRA

No, my dearest, let's not do more damage.
We've already reaped enough unhappy harvest;
let's not have yet further bloodshed.
Go back to your houses, you respected elders,
go before you suffer; yield to how things are determined.
We have done the things we had to.
If this proves the end of troubles, we would welcome that,
1660 since we've been lacerated by the Daimon's talon.
That is my woman's contribution,
in case anybody thinks it worthy of attention.

AEGISTHUS

But to have these people letting loose their tongues against me,
trying out their luck in hurling their defiance!
Should they be allowed to scorn their ruler without thinking?

CHORUS LEADER

Argives could not stoop to bow before a worthless creature.

AEGISTHUS

I shall still be looking out to get my hands on you in future.

CHORUS LEADER

Not if some divinity directs Orestes back to Argos.

AEGISTHUS

I am well aware that those in exile feed themselves on hoping.

CHORUS LEADER

All right, glut yourself, and mess with justice while you have
the chance to.

AEGISTHUS

1670 Trust me, you shall pay back dearly for this mad defiance.

CHORUS LEADER

Keep on crowing like a cock parading by his hen-bird.

CLYTEMNESTRA

Take no notice of their futile yapping.
You and I shall take control together,
and set straight the powers of this palace.

> [CLYTEMNESTRA *ushers* AEGISTHUS *and his guards into the palace. The old men of the* CHORUS *disperse in silence.*]

WOMEN AT THE GRAVESIDE

CHARACTERS

ORESTES, son of Agamemnon and Clytemnestra; he has spent
  his childhood in exile
PYLADES, companion to Orestes; son of Strophius, king of
  Phocis, who has looked after Orestes in exile
ELECTRA, older sister of Orestes; she has remained in Argos
CLYTEMNESTRA, wife and killer of Agamemnon; she has taken
  over rule in Argos with Aegisthus
CILISSA, old nurse of Orestes
AEGISTHUS, lover and now husband of Clytemnestra
SLAVE, member of the palace household
CHORUS, enslaved women, now serving the royal house at Argos

  [PLACE: *By the tomb of* AGAMEMNON *at Argos; then before the
  royal palace.*]

Scene 1

[ORESTES, *accompanied by* PYLADES, *enters; they approach
the tomb of* AGAMEMNON.]

ORESTES

I pray to Hermes of the Underworld,
custodian of my father's powers:
come, act as keeper and confederate.

(3) This is the day of my return from exile to this land,
<and, now I am become a man, the time has come
to claim my heritage and seek out my revenge.
My father, conqueror of Troy,
was cast down from his throne>by furtive trickery,
the action of a woman's hand,
<which pinioned him in lowly death.
Now, Hermes, help the dead to strengthen those who live,
and set upright once more their fallen claims.
With my loyal comrade, Pylades from Phocis>,
I stand here by my father's sepulchre,

(5) and call on him below to hear and pay me heed:
<do not lie listless in the folds of dark,
but through your son assert your power once more.
        [*Cutting two locks of hair.*]
Now that I've safely reached your tomb,
I dedicate two locks of hair, kept growing for this day.>
This one, in gratitude for nurturing my life,
I offer to the river Inachus.

(7) And second this, as token of my grief,
I place here on the stony ground,
<poor substitute for funeral-tears,>
because I was not there to mourn,

(9)   nor lay my hand upon your bier,
as your poor corpse was carried out for burial.
<But now, to judge from your neglected tomb,
no proper rites are offered here,
and so your memory becomes,
just as our enemies must hope, obscured.>

10   Look, look! What is this group of women coming near,
conspicuous in their funereal black?
Whatever should I make of this?
Could some renewed disaster have beset the house?
Or am I right to think they may be bringing
offerings to pour out to my father,
as propitiation for the dead below?
Yes, that must be the reason, for I think I see Electra,
my own sister—she stands out in anguished grief.
O Zeus, grant me due vengeance for my father's death;
be my confederate.

[ELECTRA *and the* CHORUS, *dressed in black, are by now visible.*]

20   Now, Pylades, let's stand aside from here,
so we can learn more surely why these women
are approaching for this ritual.

[*They hide.*]

Choral Song

CHORUS

Sent from the palace I come,
bearing these libations;
see how my cheeks are defaced,
red with laceration,
furrows fresh dug by my nails.
Linen robes in tatters

30 scream through the rips by my breast
    comfortless disasters.
    Hair-raising cries from a dream,
    anger gasped from slumbers,
    deep from within in the night
    roused the women's chambers,
    as it pressed hard on the house.
    God-assured soothsayers
40 cried that those under the earth
    rage against their slayers.

    Mother Earth, our birth,
    that godless woman sent me to do
    this rite that is not right,
    to try to keep her troubles at bay—
    her voice was terrified.
    For once that blood is spilled on the ground,
    what ransom can be paid?
    O hearth so overwhelmed with distress,
50 and house torn down, destroyed!
    An utter dark denied any sun,
    black dynastic hatred,
    surrounds this place in its stifling gloom,
    now that its lords lie dead.

    Respect that was unconquered, unbowed,
    has given way, distraught:
(60) yet Justice is bound to tip her scales,
    by day or dusk or night.

    Blood that's been drunk down
    by the earth, our nurse,
    sets in vengeful clots

that will not disperse.
For the guilty ones
ruin without cease
grips and riddles them
with intense disease.

Just as there's no cure
if one breaks the seals
round a virgin bed,
so if all the streams
could make confluence
to erase the stain
from murder-bloodied hands,
they still wash in vain.

When the gods enforced my city's doom,
falling to onslaught in war,
I was taken from my father's home
to live in slavery here.
So it's proper for me to approve,
whether they're just or unjust,
those who have the control of my life—
and keep abhorrence suppressed.
All the same, I hide my face behind
my cloak and secretly weep
at the senseless fates my masters bind,
my blood-flow frozen in grief.

Scene 2

ELECTRA

You servant women, keepers of our house,
since you are here to help me with this supplication,
please advise me over this:
what words am I to say while pouring out
these funeral offerings?
How speak, yet with good sense?
How pray sincerely to my father?
Am I to say, "I bring these offerings
from a loving wife to her beloved husband"—
90   those words from my mother?
I have no heart for that, yet nothing else to say
as I pour out this liquid on my father's tomb.
Or should I speak the customary words:
"May you give favor in return to those
who send these offerings, a gift to match their own"?
Or should I spill them on the ground
in silence, disrespectfully—the way my father died—
and walk away with eyes averted,
like one who throws away some pot of scourings left from
    ritual?
100   Please share in this decision with me, friends,
considering how we nurse within the house
a common hatred.
Don't conceal your thoughts through fear of anyone:
the same fate waits for both the free
and those subjected to another's rule.
So speak up if you have a better plan.

CHORUS LEADER

Since I respect your father's tomb as if it were an altar,
I shall, as prompted, speak out from the heart:
while you are pouring, utter words that favor
those who sympathize with us.

ELECTRA

110   And whom should I declare among our friends?

CHORUS LEADER

First say yourself and anyone who hates Aegisthus.

ELECTRA

What others should I add as on our side?

CHORUS LEADER

Recall Orestes—even though he is abroad.

ELECTRA

That is advice I find most welcome.

CHORUS LEADER

And as for those ones guilty of the killing . . .

ELECTRA

Explain to me, what should I say of them?

CHORUS LEADER

. . . Pray that some god or human comes to deal with them.

ELECTRA

120   You mean as judge? Or bringing justice?

CHORUS LEADER

Declare it plainly: one to kill them in their turn.

ELECTRA

Can it be right for me to ask the gods for this?

CHORUS LEADER

Of course: your enemies should pay for wrongs in kind.

ELECTRA

<I gratefully accept your words,
and now I have the confidence to pray out loud.>
O Hermes of the Underworld, please act for me,

and tell those deities beneath the ground,
who oversee my father's heritage, to listen to my prayers;
so too may Earth herself, who brings forth everything
and then receives her produce back again.
And as I pour these liquids to the dead,
130   I call upon my father now to pity me;
and let Orestes light a flame within our house.
For, as things are, we are like vagrants,
sold off by our mother, who has bought herself
a partner in exchange, I mean Aegisthus,
who's confederate, joint-guilty of your murdering.
So while I am no better than a slave,
Orestes still remains a fugitive,
far from his property; and all the while
they revel in the luxuries you labored for.
Here are my prayers for us, so listen to me, father:
may Orestes come back here by some good luck;
140   and grant that I myself may be more self-controlled
than my own mother, and more virtuous in deeds.
Against our enemies I ask for vengeance
so your killers shall be duly killed in turn.
I lay this hostile curse upon their heads:
to us, though, send good fortune,
helped by Earth and Justice who brings victory.
        [*She pours her offerings.*]
Accompanied by prayers like these,
I pour out these libations.
150   And, women, it's your place to garland them
with lamentations, and deliver hymns
restoring victory for the dead.

CHORUS [*as they pour their libations*]
>   Hear our teardrops falling
>   for our buried ruler
>   on this honored chamber,
>   shield against miasma,
>   where we pour libations.
>   Hear us, mighty sovereign,
>   hear us from the night.

[*They cry out in lament.*]

160
>   May he come, the warrior:
>   liberate this household;
>   aim his piercing arrows;
>   draw his shining sword-blade,
>   ready for the fight.

Scene 3

ELECTRA
My father has received his due libations through the earth.
[*Agitated because she has seen something.*]
But now here's something new I call on you to share.

CHORUS LEADER
Please tell—my heart leaps up with fear.

ELECTRA
Here on the tomb I've found a lock of hair.

CHORUS LEADER
What man could it have come from? Or what girl?

ELECTRA
(170) There's no one could have cut it off except myself.

CHORUS LEADER
True, those who should have mourned this way are enemies.

ELECTRA

What's more, this one looks closely similar to . . .

CHORUS LEADER

Tell me whose hair it's like.

ELECTRA

. . . it looks so very like my own.

CHORUS LEADER

You mean this is a secret offering from Orestes?

ELECTRA

It looks exactly as his hair should be.

CHORUS LEADER

But how could he have dared to journey here?

ELECTRA

180   He must have sent it as a tribute to his father.

CHORUS LEADER

This would be just as full of sorrow, if it means
he's never to set foot upon this land.

ELECTRA

A surge of anguish swells within my heart as well,
as though an arrow-point had pierced me through.
As I look on this lock of hair,
a rising flood of tears drop unrestrainedly,
I can't imagine any other Argive is responsible—
it surely cannot be the killer cut it,
190   yes, my mother (though her viciousness
toward her children hardly fits that name).
The thought that this delight comes
from the dearest person in the world—
Orestes . . . I find that wish so tempting.
Ah, if only like some messenger
it could acquire a conscious voice!
Then I would not be racked with indecision,
but be certain either to dismiss this lock

as cut off from an enemy head,
or else to think of it as kindred in my mourning,

200   homage to this tomb and honor for my father.

[*She now finds footprints and goes to step in them.*]
Look, here are footprints, a second kind of evidence—
and they are comparable to mine.
The heels and shaping of the soles

210   are in proportion with my own.
This is so agonizing, soul-destroying.

(201)   I call upon the gods: they know what sort
of tempest-storms are whirling me about.
Yet, if it is our lot to reach safe haven,

(204)   then a mighty tree may grow up from a little seed.

ORESTES [*emerging from hiding*]
Then tell the gods your prayers have met fulfillment,
and pray to win success in what is still to come.

ELECTRA
Why? What favor have the gods done for me now?

ORESTES
You're face to face with him you have been praying for.

ELECTRA
How can you know who I've been crying for?

ORESTES
I know you have been struck with wonder for Orestes.

ELECTRA
And how have I the answer to my prayers?

ORESTES
It's me. No need to search for one who's closer.

ELECTRA

220   Is this some trick you're winding round me, stranger?

ORESTES
In that case I'd be weaving plots around myself.

ELECTRA

I see: you want to mock me in my misery?

ORESTES

I'm laughing at myself, then, if I laugh at you.

ELECTRA

You really are Orestes? Is that what I should call you?

ORESTES

Now that you're looking at me in the flesh,
you find me hard to recognize,
yet when you saw this lock of hair
you were elated, and you conjured up my image
as you traced your footprints over mine.
230   Now put this curl beside where it was cut;
    [*He produces a decorated piece of cloth.*]
and look well at this cloth, the work of your own hands,
this weaving and the figure of a lion.
    [ELECTRA *embraces him.*]
Stay calm, don't let yourself be overcome with joy—
because, as I am well aware, our closest kin
are bitter enemies.

ELECTRA

You are the dearest sweetheart
of our father's house, the wept-for hope
our bloodline's seed might be preserved.
Trust in your strength
and you can yet possess our property.
To see your face!
You have to fill four roles for me: my father's,
240   then my mother's—affection I divert to you
since she is bound to have my total hatred—
and my sister's, cruelly sacrificed.
And then you are my brother,
my one true and only strength.

May Power and Justice and almighty Zeus, as third,
stand with you by your side.

ORESTES

Zeus, Zeus, look down upon these things:
see here the orphaned children of the eagle father,
who was crushed to death
within the fearsome viper's squirming coils.

250 Starvation presses heavy on the orphans
who are not full-grown enough to fetch
their father's prey back to their nesting-place.
In that way look on me and on Electra here,
bereft, and exiles from our property.

ELECTRA

He was so generous, Zeus, in sacrifices made to you.
If you abandon us, his eagle-chicks,
where will you get such splendid feasting from?
Just as you could not send trustworthy signs to mortals
if you made extinct the breed of eagles,

260 so, if this royal stock were wholly shriveled up,
it could not help to keep your altars
stocked on sacrificial days.
Provide for us and from its remnants make
this household great, though now it seems so low.

CHORUS LEADER

Hush, children, you preservers of your father's hearth,
in case someone should hear you, and through idle talk
tell everything to those in power.
One day I hope to see them torched in bubbling pitch!

ORESTES

270 Apollo's powerful oracle commanded me
to carry out this dangerous task—
it will not let me down.
It warned me loud and clear about the chilling blights

that would invade my fevered heart, were I to fail
to run to earth those guilty of my father's death
in just the way they did themselves—
which means that I must kill them in return.
It said that otherwise I'd pay with my own life,
and threatened me with many gruesome sufferings,
describing rabid fury from the vengeful powers of earth—
280   malign afflictions, greedy cankers of the flesh
that eat at healthy tissue, and of ulcers white with mold.
It told as well of other onslaughts from Erinyes
incited by a father's blood,
dark forces which unleash the weaponry
of fallen kin who beg for retribution.
Madness and night-panic fears convulse him,
290   hounding him from home, his body mutilated.
Such a one cannot participate in offering libations,
since a father's wrath debars him from all sacrificial altars;
and none will share a roof with him.
In time, devoid of rights, devoid of friends,
he dies, exhausted, desiccated.
Should I believe at all in oracles like these?
Well, even if I did not, still it must be done, the deed.
For there are many urgings which combine to this one end:
besides the god's command,
300   there is the heavy burden of my grief,
and pressure from my lack of wealth;
and I should not allow the glorious citizens of Argos,
valiant conquerors of Troy, to live on as they are,
subjected to a brace of women.

Scene 4

CHORUS

Mighty Moirai, bring fulfillment,
just as Zeus would have it. Justice,
when collecting what is owing,
shouts out: "Hate-filled language should be
310   paid with hate-filled language: so too
deadly blows should be repaid with
deadly blows." The ancient proverb
has it: *Doing leads to suffering.*

ORESTES

Father, fateful father,
what can I say, what can I do,
reaching from so far off
to where your grave-bed fetters you?
320   Light contests with darkness;
and so lament may gladden you.

CHORUS

The ravening pyre,
child, does not devour
the power of the dead.
Later they're angered;
the power which can hurt
is raised to the light.
330   Tears for the father
trace justice further.

ELECTRA

Hear this in turn, father:
cries of children by your tomb,

doubly tearful heartache.
Your grave has welcomed exiles home.
What's good? What brings no harm?
Disaster can't be overthrown.

CHORUS

340   Even so, a god may choose to
turn your song to more propitious.
Then instead of tombside dirges
we might hear a song of triumph
as it ushers through the palace
vintage that's been freshly blended.

ORESTES

I wish you had been felled at Troy,
impaled by an enemy throw.
Then you'd have left your house with fame,
your children a living so fine
350   as to turn people's eyes in the street;
your tomb-mound raised to a sight
seen over the sea from afar—
that would have been lighter to bear.

CHORUS

Under the ground
our majestic lord
is valued as dear
to the dear lords there;
360   for, king in life here,
he was honored with power,
and the scepter's sway
that all men obey.

ELECTRA

I don't even wish that beneath
Troy's walls you had gone to your death,
by Scamander's dark stream to be laid
along with the other war-dead.
I'd rather that murderous pair
had met with their doom far from here,
370   and that I'd heard they were gone,
without ever knowing this pain.

CHORUS

What you speak of, daughter, would be
better far than gold or fortune—
but it's nothing more than wishing.
Yet this double scourge cracks nearer:
all your allies lie in Hades,
while usurpers live and rule with
hands polluted, bringing shame on
both the father and his children.

ORESTES

380   That pierces me right through
like an arrow shot.
Zeus, Zeus, send from below,
though it may come late,
punishment to fall
upon those violent brutes,
to pay my father full
all they owe in debts.

CHORUS

Oh for the chance to sing out,
raising my jubilant cries
over the man as he's struck,

over the wife as she dies.

390   Why should I try to hide these
wing-beats perturbing my heart?
Bitter winds drive on my soul,
squall-blasts of furious hate.

ELECTRA

Almighty Zeus, when shall
you bring down your hand
to split apart their skulls?
That would assure this land.
I pray that justice shall
displace what is unjust.
I ask you, Earth, to hear,
and powers below, assist.

CHORUS

400   There's a rule that lays it down that
spattering of life-blood spilling
on the ground must summon further
bloodshed. Murder calls upon an
Erinys to draw on deadly
retribution for the murdered.

ORESTES

O you rulers of the underworld,
and you powerful curses of the dead,
see this residue of Atreus' blood,
helpless and deprived of heritage.
Tell us which way's best to turn, O Zeus.

410   CHORUS

Now my heart too is disturbed,
hearing this pitiful claim,
and I'm diminished in hope,

my inner parts darkened with gloom
by the dismay you reveal.
When, though, you're strong in your call,
boldness dislodges my hurt,
urging that all will be well.

ELECTRA

What would be most convincing for our claim?
How our mother has inflicted pain?
420   She may stroke, but cannot make us calm,
since my heart is like a savage wolf,
deadened to a mother's touch by wrath.

CHORUS

I have beaten my breast
to the beat of the Arian drum;
I have sung my lament
to the strains of the Kissian dirge,
with hands clutching my hair,
and with spattering blood thick as rain,
with hands clattering down
from above, drumming loud in my brain.

ELECTRA

430   O mother, cruel-minded,
you made his cruel interment:
a king without his people,
without his proper weeping.
So heartlessly you buried
your husband, unlamented.

ORESTES

You tell of gross insult:
well, she must pay the sum
for bringing this insult

against our father's name,
with help from the gods,
with help from my strength.
Then, when I've done with her,
I'll gladly suffer death.

CHORUS

440

She amputated parts
from him; she who did that
in that state buried him,
eager to make his fate
unbearable for you
to live with all your days.
So now you've learned of how
your father was disgraced.

ELECTRA

You tell of his lowly death.
I was kept well away in disgrace,
counted as of no worth,
kenneled prisoner deep in the house,
like some dangerous cur,
where my tears of grief secretly fell.
Now you've heard how it was,

450

mark it deeply incised on your soul.

CHORUS

Yes, listen and inscribe it;
drill your ear to absorb it.
This is the way things are now:
next rouse the passion to know
the future. And join battle
with unbending mettle.

ORESTES

    Father, I call: join our cause.

ELECTRA

    Through my tears I add my voice.

CHORUS

    We add this cry sent from all:
    hear us straight, come to this light,
460   help us face those whom we hate.

ORESTES

    Fight meets fight, right confronts right.

ELECTRA

    Gods, carry through what is just.

CHORUS

    I tremble to hear your prayer.
    Too long has fate had to wait:
    may it respond to our prayers.

    O pain bred in the house,
    and discordant notes
    of Ruin's bloody strokes,
    lamentable woes
    impossible to bear,
470   difficult to close.
    The house must find a way
    to redress its wound,
    not helped by outside hand,
    but by inbred feud.
    The gods below chant out
    this refrain of blood.

CHORUS LEADER

    Listen, blessed chthonic spirits,
    send your help with ready favor
    to the children: let them triumph.

Scene 5

ORESTES

My father, brought low in a manner so unfitting for a king,
480   grant my request to be the master of your heritage.

ELECTRA

My father, I have this demand as well:
to overthrow Aegisthus and to win a home.

ORESTES

For only then will there be feasting in your name;
or else you'll be deprived among the dead
when they are celebrated with burnt sacrifice.

ELECTRA

And I shall bring drink-offerings on my wedding day,
drawn from the dowry of our house.
And I'll revere this tomb above all others.

ORESTES

O Earth, send up my father; let him oversee our fight.

ELECTRA

490   Persephone, bestow on us his power in all its splendor.

ORESTES

Do not forget the bath where you were hacked to death.

ELECTRA

Do not forget the trap-net they invented.

ORESTES

You were snared in fetters, though not bronze.

ELECTRA

Trussed up inside a cowardly covering.

ORESTES

Do these humiliations rouse you from your sleep?

ELECTRA

And are you lifting up your much-loved head?

ORESTES

Send Justice as an ally to your friends;
or give us strength to get a grip as strong as theirs,
if, after your defeat, you want to wrest back victory.

ELECTRA

500 And, father, hear this final call for help:
see here these chicks of yours, perched on your tomb.
Take pity on the crying of the female and the male.

ORESTES

And don't wipe out the seed of this bloodline.

ELECTRA

And then, though dead, you won't have wholly died.

ORESTES

For children keep a man's repute still living after death;
like corks, they hold the net afloat,
and stop the flaxen web from sinking down.

ELECTRA

Hear us: for you we raise up our lament.

ORESTES

If you support our claims, you will preserve yourself.

CHORUS LEADER

510 It is quite right you have expressed yourselves at length
to make up for the lack of mourning at this tomb.
But next, since you are firmly set on deeds,
it is high time to start, and try your fate.

ORESTES

You're right. But first, to keep on track,
I need to know just why she sent libations here.
What was the point in trying—far too late—
to make amends and heal that trauma too far gone for cure?
I see no sense in offering such a futile favor to the dead.

The gifts are far too paltry for the crime—
520 for as the proverb says, "Pour everything you have
to pay for one man's blood, it's labor wasted."
So if you know the reason, please enlighten me.

CHORUS LEADER

I know, my child, since I was there.
It was bad dreams and terrors of the night that shook
that godless woman into sending these libations.

ORESTES

And did you find out what this dream was all about?

CHORUS LEADER

She dreamt, she said, of giving birth . . . but to a snake.

ORESTES

Where does this story lead? How does it end?

CHORUS LEADER

She wrapped it tight with cloth, just like a child.

ORESTES

530 What sort of feeding did it want, this new-born creature?

CHORUS LEADER

Within her dream she offered her own breast.

ORESTES

But was her nipple not then punctured by its fangs?

CHORUS LEADER

It sucked out clots of blood mixed with her milk.
She woke in terror, screaming,
and the many household lamps, that had been blotted
by the dark, flared up to serve our mistress.
Then she sent these grave-libations in the hope
that they might work to cut out her disease.

ORESTES

540 Well then I pray to Earth here and my father's tomb
to bring this dream to pass for me.
I offer this interpretation, one that fits it closely:

the snake emerged from that same place as me;
it latched onto the breast that once fed me;
it drew sweet milk yet curdled with her blood;
she screamed in horror at all this.
So it must be that, as she nourished this monstrosity,
so must she die by violence.
And I, turned snake . . . I am to kill her.
550 That is what the dream proclaims.

CHORUS LEADER

Yes, I approve your reading of this omen—
may it turn out true.
And now tell us, your friends, about what still remains—
who should be taking action, and who not.

ORESTES

The plan is simple. First Electra here should go inside.
I urge on you and her to keep our plotting secret.
That way those who slaughtered a great man by stealth
shall be themselves entrapped by stealth,
and die in the same noose,
just as Apollo told in prophecy.
560 I shall myself approach the outer gateway,
looking like a stranger, kitted out with baggage;
I'll bring Pylades along with me,
our family's closest ally, and we'll imitate
the dialect that's spoken in his land of Phocis.
And then if none of those who man the doors
will open up to us in friendly fashion—
since this house contains malignity—
we shall stay put just as we are,
so anybody passing by will speculate and say,
"Now, why's Aegisthus keeping new arrivals at the gate,
570 if he's indoors and knows of them?"
But if I once get past the outer gates

and find him sitting on my father's throne,
or if he comes and gives me audience,
then, just as soon as I set eyes on him—
before he has the time to say,
"Where is the stranger from?"—
I'll make a corpse of him, impaled on my swift blade.
Then the Erinys—hardly short of blood—
will drink a third, unblended cup.
    [To ELECTRA.]
Now you go in and keep good watch
580 around the house, so things are organized to fit.
    [To the CHORUS.]
And you I would advise to keep your tongue discreet,
keep silent when you should, and speak to fit the moment.
In all else, I call on Hermes to keep watch,
and make this contest of the sword go well for me.
    [ORESTES and PYLADES go off.]

Choral Song

CHORUS

    The earth produces
    many fearsome beasts and terrors,
    the sea embraces
    seething shoals of dreadful monsters.
590   The sudden flashes
    flaring through the earth and heavens
    inflict their dangers
    on both winged and walking creatures;
    and there's the damage
    dealt by furious blasts of tempests.

But these are nothing
set beside harm done by people—
by men through daring
and the recklessness of women,
who partner ruin
through their dangerous emotions.
The female-ruling
power of illicit passion
breaks the union
that binds humans into households.

Everyone should know the tale of
how Althaea killed her son
Meleager, when she cruelly
carried through her deadly plan:
how she took the blood-red timber,
placed it on a new-lit fire,
burned the log that shared his life span
ever since his first birth-cry
when he issued from her belly,
matched in time with him exactly
up until his dying day.

There's another hateful story
tells how deadly Scylla's greed
handed into hostile clutches
him most close to her by blood.
She was tempted by the necklace,
spellbound by its golden look,
so she cut her father Nisus'
death-denying magic lock.
As he slept all unsuspecting,
he was sent to Hades' dark.

—

The crime of the women of Lemnos
is foulest of all these deeds;
they ruthlessly murdered their husbands
deserting to other beds.
Comparing all of these ruthless
atrocities from the past,
there's not one surpasses the coupling
this household detests the worst:
the treacherous plot of a woman
who murdered her warrior lord,
(630)   and sleeps with another. I value
the wife who remains subdued.

(640)   So stand up for Justice in the fight
when trampled down underfoot;
safeguard the solemn power of Zeus
from those attempting abuse.
Justice is rooted firm, and Fate
is eager to forge the blade,
bringing a child inside the gate
650   to get crimes of past blood paid.
She'll finally claim her dues
through the brooding Erinys.

Scene 6

[ORESTES, *accompanied by* PYLADES, *enters from the side,
goes to the door, and knocks.*]

ORESTES
    Hello there! Slave!
    Can you not hear my knocking at the outer gates?
      [*Knocks again.*]

Is someone there?

Hey, Slave, once more—who's there inside?

[*Knocks again.*]

Three times I've called for someone to come out—

if, that is, this palace of Aegisthus offers hospitality.

SLAVE [*emerging from inside*]

All right, all right, I hear you!

Where's the stranger from?

ORESTES

Please tell the masters of the house

that I have come to bring them news.

660 And hurry up—night's dusky chariot is drawing near,

and it's high time for traders to be dropping anchor

in a friendly house of welcome.

Fetch out someone who's in charge—

the mistress of the house . . .

or more appropriate would be the man,

since courtesies inhibit what can be expressed,

whereas in conversation man-to-man

one can be bold and say just what one means.

CLYTEMNESTRA [*entering*]

Please tell me, strangers, what you want.

We have available the kind of comforts

that are proper for a household of this standing:

670 hot baths, and beds to soothe out weariness,

and honest company.

But if there's any further business needing

serious discussion, then that's men's work,

and we shall pass it on to them.

ORESTES

I am a Daulian from Phocis.

As I was setting out for Argos,

loaded with my baggage on my back,

I met up with a man, unknown to me and me to him.
He, when he had inquired about my destination, said
—this Strophius, as I learned that he was called—
680   he said, "Well, since you're bound for Argos, stranger,
please remember this exactly,
and convey it to his parents: say to them,
'Orestes is gone, dead'—
make sure you get that right.
Find if his family prefers to fetch him home,
or have him buried far away for evermore;
and bring me their instructions on this choice.
An urn of bronze already holds within its sides
the ashes of the man—he has been well lamented."
I have told you what I heard.
I do not know if I am speaking with some relatives;
690   but it is only right to let his parents know.

CLYTEMNESTRA

Such pain! This spells complete destruction!
O you curse upon this house, so hard to overthrow,
you spy on all, including those put out of reach of harm.
From far you still bring down with your unerring arrows
all my dearest kin, and strip me bare.
And now Orestes, who was carefully avoiding paths
that brought him near the deadly quagmire. . . .
But the brightest hope that there would be
a healer for the fever-frenzy in our house . . .
set down that hope as dashed.

ORESTES

700   I would have wished it might have been
for some good news I'd come to be received
by hosts so prosperous as you—
since host and guest is such a warm relationship.
But all the same I would have felt it impious

not to have completely carried through
a matter such as this, once I'd agreed to it.

CLYTEMNESTRA

You'll not be treated any less deservingly,
nor be less welcome in this house—
some other person would have brought this message.

710   But it's time for guests who have been traveling far all day
to be made comfortable.

　　[*To Attendant.*]

Escort him and this fellow-trader
to the men's guest rooms, and let them have
whatever's proper for this house.
And I'll convey these matters to the masters of the house;
we are not short of friends
with whom we can discuss this sad event.

　　[ORESTES *and* PYLADES *are taken into the palace;* CLYTEMNESTRA
　　also goes in.]

Choral Chant

CHORUS

　　　　When, dear fellow servants, when shall
720　　　　we be able to proclaim our
　　　　voices fully for Orestes?
　　　　Mighty Earth and mighty grave mound
　　　　heaped upon our royal commander's
　　　　corpse, now listen, and now help us.
　　　　Now's the moment for Persuasion
　　　　slyly to conspire with Hermes,
　　　　and to steer this trial by sword blade.

Scene 7

[*The old nurse,* CILISSA, *comes out of the palace in distress.*]

CHORUS LEADER

730 It looks as though that stranger has been
    making trouble: I can see the aged nursemaid
    of Orestes here, reduced to tears.
    Where are you heading from the palace gates, Cilissa,
    with sorrow as your unhired fellow-traveler?

CILISSA

    Aegisthus—the mistress has commanded me
    to fetch him here as quick as possible
    to meet the strangers, and to find out more
    about this new report by talking man to man.
    In front of servants she put on a gloomy face,
    but she was laughing secretly inside.
    For her, events have turned out well,
740 although disastrous for this house—
    that's what the strangers have made clear.
    When that man hears the tale, he's going to be delighted.
    The old misfortune-mixture in this house of Atreus
    was quite hard enough and pained me to the heart,
    but never have I had to suffer such a blow as this.
    I had to drain the dregs of all those other troubles,
    but for dear Orestes . . .
    the one who wore me out, the one I cared for
750 from the day that I received him from his mother . . .
    How often I was made to get up in the night,
    awakened by his piercing cries,
    and had to put up with unpleasant tasks—
    and all for nothing.

It has to be a nurse's job to cater
for a creature with no words.
A little one in baby clothes can't say
what is the matter: whether it is hunger or else thirst,
or other business—a baby's bowels and bladder
have a willpower of their own.
I've had to try and prophesy—and often got it wrong,
and so become a laundress of baby clothes,
760   both nurse and washer-woman rolled in one.
I carried out this task to raise Orestes for his father's sake.
And now I hear that he is dead.
I have to go and fetch the man
who has defiled this house.
And he'll be all too glad to hear this news.

CHORUS LEADER

What kind of crew did she tell him to bring?

CILISSA

What do you mean? Explain more clearly.

CHORUS LEADER

To come with bodyguards, or on his own?

CILISSA

She said to bring his full-armed escort.

CHORUS LEADER

770   In that case, do not pass that message
to our hated master: but put on instead a cheerful front,
and tell him he should come as quickly as he can,
and that he has no need to be afraid.
The one who takes a message can contrive
to make a crooked word sound straight.

CILISSA

But how can you be happy with this news?

CHORUS LEADER

Supposing Zeus might turn our troubles round. . . .

CILISSA

How so? Our greatest hope Orestes is no more.

CHORUS LEADER

Don't be too quick. That could turn out a poor prediction.

CILISSA

What? Do you know of something different?

CHORUS LEADER

Go, give your message in the form we've told you.

780   The gods take care of what they care about.

CILISSA

All right. I'll do as you have said.

God willing, may all turn out for the best.

[*Exit* CILISSA.]

Choral Song

CHORUS

Father Zeus, now hear our pleas:
grant this house may gain success.
Bring for those who wish it well
the sight they long for in its hall.
Zeus, fulfill our prayers:
help the man inside
to crush his enemies.
790   If you help him rise,
he'll heap recompense,
twice and thrice as high.
Ready by the chariot-
yoke he stands, the orphan colt,
son of him you highly prized—
set good rhythm to his stride.

———

You gods who guard the wealth
stored deep in the house,
now hear and sympathize;
lend strength and join our cause,
to clear away the blood
of crimes done long ago.
Bring justice, so old grudge
may no more multiply.
Revive, Apollo, here
the light of freedom's flame,
and help it to shine from
behind the veil of gloom.
May Hermes join what's just:
with slanting words awry
he may spread darkness, yet
be no more clear by day.

And then at last we'll sing,
to help the house sail free,
our full-voiced female song,
our breath a following breeze.
But you be brave and true
when action takes its turn:
when she cries out, "My son,"
shout back, "My father's son."
That way you'll bring to pass
a ruin that's no wrong.
Put Perseus in your heart
to shear the Gorgon's head,
and sprinkle blood to blight
for good the murder-seed.

Scene 8

[*Enter* AEGISTHUS, *by himself.*]

AEGISTHUS

I have been summoned here, and here I am.

840   I gather that some strangers have arrived
with far from welcome news about Orestes' death,
a blow to set the blood fresh dripping in this house,
still raw and oozing from the earlier killing.
What is this, then? Should I regard it as the actual truth?
Or is it merely women's panic-talk,
which sends sparks flying up that then die out?
What can you tell me that might clear my mind?

CHORUS LEADER

We've heard of it. But you should go inside
and find out from the visitors yourself.
Reported news is nowhere near as good

850   as learning from the messenger direct.

AEGISTHUS

I want to meet and ask him if he was himself
nearby the day Orestes died.
Or is he merely passing on a distant rumor?
He'll not fool a mind that keeps its wits awake.

[*Exit* AEGISTHUS *into the palace.*]

Choral Chant

CHORUS

    Zeus, Zeus, where should I begin my
    prayers and pleading? Where to end them?

860 Now the bloodstained slashing blades are
either just about to snuff for-
ever Agamemnon's family,
or to light the flame of freedom,
and to pass the city's power and
riches over to Orestes.
That's the contest he is joining
singlehanded with a double
rival. May he be victorious.

Scene 9

[*A death-cry is heard from inside.*]

CHORUS LEADER

870 Ah! What's happening? What's the outcome?
Let us keep our distance while the issue is decided,
so we seem quite free of blame.
It's clear the battle has now been decided.

SLAVE [*hurrying out*]

Ah, ah! Disaster, help!
The master's been attacked.
Ah! help! I call again.
Aegisthus lives no more!
Open the doors as quickly as you can;
unbolt the women's quarters too.
We need a strong young man—

880 yet that won't help the one who's been dispatched.
Help, help! I'm calling on deaf ears,
I'm yelling pointlessly at people fast asleep.
Where's Clytemnestra gone? What is she at?

CHORUS LEADER

It looks as though her neck is on the block,
about to be hacked through by Justice.

CLYTEMNESTRA [*entering hastily*]
  What's going on here?
  Why raise this alarm?
SLAVE
  I say the dead are slaughtering the living.
CLYTEMNESTRA
  Ah, I see the meaning of your riddle:
  we're about to die by trickery, just as we killed.
  Quick, someone fetch an ax that's good to kill a man.
890 Let's see if we shall conquer or be conquered—
  since that's the dreadful depth that we have reached.
     [ORESTES *enters with* PYLADES *from inside.*]
ORESTES
  It's you I'm looking for: this one has had enough.
CLYTEMNESTRA
  Oh, are you dead, Aegisthus, my dear love?
ORESTES
  You love the man? In that case you can lie
  beside him in a double grave—
  that way you'll never be unfaithful, even not in death.
CLYTEMNESTRA [*baring her breast*]
  —Stop there, my son!
  Now feel restraint, my child, before this breast of mine,
  where often drowsily with toothless gums
  you used to suck at the nutritious milk.
ORESTES
  What should I do now, Pylades,
  should I hold back from striking my own mother dead?
PYLADES
900 What then to make in future of Apollo's
  Delphic oracles, and of our sacred oaths?
  Treat any human as your enemy before the gods.

ORESTES

I judge you win, and your advice is good.

[*Turning back to* CLYTEMNESTRA.]

Now come with me—I want to kill you at his side,
considering you rated him above my father still alive.
Now you can go to bed with him in death,
the man you loved, while filled with loathing
for the one you should have loved.

CLYTEMNESTRA

I nourished you when young: I want to age with you.

ORESTES

You killed my father, yet you think to live with me?

CLYTEMNESTRA

910   What-must-be shares responsibility, my child.

ORESTES

Then what-must-be lays down your death as well.

CLYTEMNESTRA

Have you no dread before a mother's curse, my child?

ORESTES

No, since you bore me only to abandon me.

CLYTEMNESTRA

I sent you to an allied house—that's not abandoning.

ORESTES

I was free-born, and yet you sold me off.

CLYTEMNESTRA

So where's the price that I received for that?

ORESTES

I feel ashamed to put that plainly into words.

CLYTEMNESTRA

So should you be to list your father's dallyings.

ORESTES

Don't criticize the man who toiled while you sat snug.

CLYTEMNESTRA

920   It's hard for wives when separated from their man.

ORESTES

The man's hard labor keeps their women safe at home.

CLYTEMNESTRA

It seems you mean to kill your mother, then.

ORESTES

It's you, not me, inflicting your own killing.

CLYTEMNESTRA

Look out: beware a mother's rabid hunting dogs.

ORESTES

How could I then escape my father's if I were to fail?

CLYTEMNESTRA

It seems I'm pointlessly lamenting to a tomb.

ORESTES

Because my father's blood decrees your death.

CLYTEMNESTRA

Ah, this . . . this is the snake I bore and fed.

My horror at that dream has proved prophetic.

ORESTES

930   You killed as you should not have:

so now suffer what you should not.

[ORESTES *takes* CLYTEMNESTRA *inside*.]

CHORUS LEADER

I sorrow even for their double fate.

But now Orestes has advanced these

many bloodsheds to their crisis point,

our choice is that the bright hope of the house

should not fall utterly destroyed.

Choral Song

CHORUS

There came to the race of Priam
harsh-punishing justice at last;
there comes, though, to Agamemnon's
palace a two-footed lion.
940   And oracles sent from Apollo
encourage the exile's brave quest.
Let us raise up our triumph-cries
for the rescuing of our house
from the draining of its riches
by that pair of tainted leeches.
To help there came Hermes, the subtle
tactician of devious battle;
(950)   alongside Justice, Zeus' daughter,
whose anger withers the guilty.

(960)   Clear we can see the light,
now the muzzle's been unbound.
So rise, our house, stand upright,
too long you've lain on the ground.
Soon our ruling lord
shall come out through this door,
once pollution has
(970)   been cleansed, and all made pure.

Scene 10

[ORESTES *is revealed standing over the bodies of* CLYTEMNESTRA
and AEGISTHUS; *his bloodstained hands hold a sword and an
olive bough.*]

ORESTES

Look, see this pair of tyrants,
killers of my father, looters of my heritage.
They were once so majestic sitting on their thrones,
and even now they still stay close,
and faithful to their promises.
They swore together to contrive my father's death,
and swore to die together—and their oath holds good.
[*Points to the robe-net that was used to trap* AGAMEMNON.]

980 Now look in turn, you witnesses of these dark things,
see this contraption, shackle for my wretched father.

(997) What might I call it, striking proper terms?
A trap? A coffin-drape to wrap a corpse
from head to foot? Or, no, a net,
a snare, a shawl for snagging ankles.
It's the sort of thing a highwayman might use,
who spends his time in tricking travelers—

(1004) with this he could enjoy dispensing death.
[*To his attendants.*]

(983) Stand round and stretch it out, this man-cloak;
display it so the father may look down on it—
not mine, I mean the father who is overseer of everything—
so he might come one day to witness for me
that with justice I pursued this deed,
my mother's death.
I don't speak of Aegisthus, since he's simply paid

990 the penalty that's laid down for adulterers.
But as for her . . . she who deployed this hateful thing
against her husband, him whose offspring
she had carried in her womb—
once loved, but now her deadly enemies—
what can you think of her?
She is more like a sea-snake or a viper
that could make a person putrefy by touch alone,
not even by her bite, just by audacity and malice.
I pray I never have that kind of wife to share my house:
I'd rather that the gods destroyed me childless first.

CHORUS

Such dreadful deeds!
She was struck down
in gruesome death.
Ah, ah!
For him still here,
pain starts to flower.

ORESTES

1010 Did she commit the deed, or did she not?
This cloak here is my witness,
dipped and dyed by stabbings from Aegisthus' sword.
The seeps of blood, combined with time,
have spoiled the many colors of its ornament.
As I address this woven cloth that killed my father,
I can now lament him, and now speak in praise.
I sorrow for what has been done,
and for the anguish, and the entire dynasty.
This victory brings stains that none can envy.

CHORUS

There's no one lives
all through their life
exempt from grief.

        Ah, ah!

        Here's present harm,

1020   and more to come.

ORESTES

I've no idea where this will end:

I'm like a charioteer

whose horses are careering off the track.

My mind is bolting uncontrollably,

and Fear is straining at my heart

to start a song and dance in step with Rage.

So while I have my wits, I make this declaration:

I struck home with justice when I killed my mother,

that polluting, god-detested killer of my father.

My incitement to take on this action

1030   was Apollo's Delphic oracle, which told me

I would be exempt from guilt if I did this,

while if I failed to do so . . .

I won't describe the punishment,

for no one could fire close to such a pitch of agony.

So now, as you can see, I'm setting off,

equipped with this wreathed olive bough,

toward Apollo's shrine, the navel of the earth,

with its undying flame, in order to escape

from inbred bloodshed.

Apollo told me to take refuge at his altar and no other.

1040   I call upon the whole of Argos to bear witness

for me in due course, and to recall

how these sad horrors came about.

But now I go, a wandering fugitive

excluded from this land.

CHORUS LEADER

But what you have achieved is good.

Don't tie your speech with words that are ill-omened.

You have freed the whole domain of Argos
by your slicing off this pair of serpents' heads.

ORESTES [*reacting with alarm as he sees a "vision"*]

Ah, look! These gruesome women here,
like Gorgons, with their gloomy robes,
and thickly wreathed around with snakes.
I cannot stay—I have to go.

CHORUS LEADER

What are they, these illusions whirling you about?
Stand firm; don't yield to fear when you have won so much.

ORESTES

These torments aren't illusions. I see clearly now:
these are my mother's rabid dogs.

CHORUS LEADER

This is because there's blood still wet upon your hands:
that's spreading this confusion in your mind.

ORESTES

O lord Apollo, here they come in swarms.
And from their eyes they drip disgusting blood and pus.

CHORUS LEADER

There's only one way to be cleansed:
Apollo's touch will free you from these torments.

ORESTES

You cannot see them, but I do.
They hunt me down.
There is no way that I can stay—I have to go.

[ORESTES *rushes away.*]

CHORUS LEADER

Good luck go with you then.
I pray the gods take care of you,
whatever may arise.

CHORUS

Now this tempest is the third to
rage and leave behind its wake of
wreckage through the royal palace.
First there was that cruel banquet:
children swallowed by their father.
1070   Second was the royal commander's
downfall, bathtub-slaughtered.
Thirdly now a kind of savior
has arrived . . . or should I call him
more a death knell? Where shall all this
reach an ending? Where be soothed to
calm, this cyclone of disaster?
[*The* CHORUS *depart into the palace.*]

ORESTES AT ATHENS

CHARACTERS

PYTHIA, the priestess in charge of the oracle of Apollo at Delphi

ORESTES, fleeing in exile after killing his mother Clytemnestra

APOLLO

CLYTEMNESTRA, appearing as a dream-ghost to the sleeping
  Chorus

ATHENA

CHORUS of Erinyes (See p. xxx)

SECONDARY CHORUS of women who look after the cult of Athena
  at Athens

[PLACE: *The entrance to the Temple of Apollo at Delphi;
moving to the site of the ancient statue of Athena on the
Acropolis at Athens; then shifting to the Areopagus Hill
nearby.*]

Scene 1

[Enter PYTHIA *from the side.*]

PYTHIA

In these my prayers I honor firstly Gaia,
the primeval prophetess;
then Themis, who was second to possess
this place, her mother's oracle.
The third to take it—by consent, no use of violence—
was another daughter born of Earth, named Phoebe;
she next gave it as a birth-gift to Apollo,
who now has the further name of Phoebus.
He, when he had left the rocks and lake of Delos,
10   made first landfall on Athena's coast;
and the Athenians escorted him with reverence
on his journey to this place beneath Parnassus.
They pioneered a sacred way from there
by civilizing lands that had been savage.
The people of this country and their ruler, Delphos,
honored him on his arrival.
Zeus inspired him with the power of prophecy,
and settled him, as Loxias, to be the fourth upon this throne.
20   These are the gods I name as prelude to my prayers.
Then next Athena-before-Delphi takes the pride of place.
And I pay homage to the Nymphs of the Corycian cavern,
favorite haunt for birds, frequented by the gods.
And let me not forget that Dionysus holds this upland,
ever since he led an army of his bacchants here
to weave a fatal trap round Pentheus, like a hare.
I call as well upon the river Pleistus;
and on great Poseidon;

and on Zeus supreme, who brings completion.

(30)   After this I go inside to take my seat as prophetess.

If there be any Greeks here present,

let them now consult,

as drawn in order by the customary lot.

for I deliver prophecies as guided by the god.

> [*She goes in; there is an empty stage before she comes*
> *stumbling back out.*]

Oh terrible! terrible to tell, to see . . .

horrors so foul they force me back outside the shrine,

and drain my strength so I can't stand,

reduced to crawling on my hands and knees—

a terrified old woman is a nothing . . . no more than a child.

As I am entering the inner sanctum,

40   there I see beside the sacred navel-stone

a man who's taken refuge as a suppliant,

his hands polluted with still-dripping blood:

in one he holds a naked sword, the other

grasps an olive-bough entwined with wool.

About him, fast asleep, there lie

the strangest band of women—not women really,

more like Gorgons . . . but then not Gorgons either. . . .

I did once see such beings in a painting,

50   pilfering the feast of Phineus.

But these ones have no wings, and are pitch black,

and utterly repulsive, reeking with disgusting snorts,

and from their eyes there drips revolting ooze.

Their whole appearance is not right for bringing near

the shrines of gods, nor human houses either.

I never have set eyes upon this race of creatures,

and I've no idea what country could

have bred them without damage or regret.

60   From now, though, it's the master of this temple

has to be responsible for this—mighty Apollo.
He is the healer, prophet, seer, and purifier.
  [PYTHIA *goes off to the side she came from.*]

Scene 2

[*Enter* APOLLO *and* ORESTES.]

ORESTES

(85)   My lord Apollo, as you know how negligence is wrong,
so too you must find out how not to be unjust.
It is your strength that is my reassurance.

APOLLO

(88)   Remember that, and don't let terror swamp your mind.
I'll not betray you, but protect you through and through,
both standing close, and from far off.
And I shall not be soft toward your enemies:
as you see now, these crazy females
have been overcome, plunged deep in slumber—
these abominations, ancient maidens, virgin crones.
No god gets close involved with them,
70   nor man, nor animal of any kind.
They cultivate the evil dark of Tartarus beneath the earth,
detested by both humans and the higher gods.
Yet, all the same, you have to flee; and show no weakness,
as they're going to drive you over seas and lands.
Don't let this struggle weary you,
but keep right on until you reach Athena's city,
80   and then stay, your arms about her ancient statue.
There we'll search out judges and beguiling words
which will ensure you are released from this distress
for all of future time—because I was the one
persuaded you to strike your mother dead.

I call upon you, Hermes, brother sharing
the same father's blood: take care of him,
90   and faithful to your title, be the guide and shepherd
to my suppliant here; and bring him,
with the help of people that he meets, good fortune.
          [APOLLO *goes into the temple;* ORESTES *sets off in haste.*]

Scene 3

[*The ghost of* CLYTEMNESTRA *enters from the temple and
speaks back to the Erinyes, who are sleeping inside.*]

CLYTEMNESTRA

Sleep on! Sleep on!
Hey! What's the use of you asleep?
Meanwhile, as long as I'm disdained by you like this,
I stay denounced among the dead by those I killed.
And so I wander in humiliation, held to blame
because, although I have been made
100   to suffer horribly by my own closest kin,
there is not one divinity enraged on my behalf,
not even for me butchered at my children's hands.
Just bring yourselves to see these gashes in my breast!
Yet you have lapped up many offerings
that I have poured unmixed with wine;
and I have burned rich sacrifices for you in the night—
a ritual time not shared with any other god.
110   I see all this go trampled underfoot,
while he has managed to escape.
Like some young deer, he's lightly bounded off
right from inside your nets, and boldly leers at you.
Hear me—it is my very self at stake.
Pay me attention, chthonic goddesses:

this dream that summons you is
Clytemnestra, me!
    [*Moaning noises from the Erinyes.*]
Yes, go on moaning!
But meanwhile the man has got away.
120   [*More moaning noises.*]
You're fast asleep, and feel no pity for my pain.
I am the mother that Orestes killed—he's got away.
    [*Crying-out noises from the Erinyes.*]
You cry aloud, yet stay asleep. Get up, I tell you.
What's your function other than inflicting pain?
    [*More crying-out noises.*]
Exhaustion joined in league with sleep
has drained the menace of your snakes.

CHORUS [*with redoubled moaning noises and cries*]
130   Get him! Get him! Get him! Get him!
Look, here's the trail!

CLYTEMNESTRA

You run in hot pursuit of your dream-prey
with yelping like a dog intent upon the chase.
Yet you are doing nothing!
Get up, I tell you!
Don't let weariness subdue your power;
don't let slumber lull you senseless.
Feel stabbing in your guts from my reproaches,
blast him with your bloody breath,
and shrivel him with scorching from your womb.
Go after him; once more pursue, and bleed him dry.
    [*The dream-ghost goes; the* CHORUS *begin to wake each other
    and to enter in disarray.*]

Choral Entry Song

140   Wake up!
And you wake her.
And I wake you.
What, still asleep?
Get up!
Kick slumber off.
Let's find out
if this prelude points to deeds.
[*Cries of anguish on finding* ORESTES *gone.*]
     Sisters, we have suffered,
     labored hard for nothing,
     suffered pain unhealing,
     wrong beyond all bearing.
     He's escaped the trap-net,
     and the beast has bolted.
     We've been caught out napping,
     and have lost our quarry.
     Son of Zeus, Apollo,
     you have played the robber.
150   You, the young, have ridden
     over gods so agèd.
     Bowing to the godless
     killer of his mother,
     you have been his cover.
     Who could call this justice?

     Reproachful dreams interrupted sleep,
     blows like a charioteer's keen whip,

160 reaching my innards, and stinging sharp.
Like being flogged in a public place,
I felt it biting as cold as ice.
This is the way they abuse what's right,
these younger gods, who defile with blood
the sacred oracle head to foot,
smearing the earth's central navel-stone
with indelibly filthy stain.

The prophet has polluted
the hearth of his own house,
170 self-prompted, self-invited;
and wrecked the gods' own laws,
rights that are deep-rooted.
But never shall he free him;
that man shall not escape,
and down below earth even
his guilt shall keep him trapped—
revenge shall still consume him.

Scene 4

[*Enter* APOLLO *from the temple.*]

APOLLO
Out! Out, I tell you!
Leave this shrine immediately
180 and void the inner chamber of the oracle:
or you'll be pierced through by a silver fang
sent flashing from my golden bow,
and that will make you fetch up livid bile,
and spew the human blood that you have swilled.
This temple's not a proper place for you:

you should be rather where men's heads
are severed, eyes are gouged;
where boys' virility is mangled by castration;
where there's amputation, stoning,

190   and men moan as they die slowly through impalement.
D'you hear the kind of god-detested
entertainment you take pleasure in?
Your whole appearance makes this obvious:
such creatures should by rights
live in a flesh-devouring lions' den,
and not be smearing their defilement round this oracle.
Be on your way, then, herd without a shepherd;
there's no god who wants to tend a flock like yours.

CHORUS LEADER

Now, lord Apollo, listen in your turn.
You are yourself no mere accomplice,

200   you're the agent bearing full responsibility.

APOLLO

What do you mean? Just tell me that.

CHORUS LEADER

It was your oracle that told the man to kill his mother?

APOLLO

I gave an oracle that told him to avenge his father, yes.

CHORUS LEADER

Then promised to protect him, though still smeared with
     blood?

APOLLO

I told him to take refuge at this shrine.

CHORUS LEADER

And yet you still abuse us when we form his escort?

APOLLO

Because you are not fit to enter in this place.

CHORUS LEADER

But this role is the one assigned to us.

APOLLO

What can this function be, this fine prerogative?

CHORUS LEADER

210   We harry mother-killers from their homes.

APOLLO

And what about a woman who cuts down her man?

CHORUS LEADER

Ah, that would not be spilling her own kindred blood.

APOLLO

That means you rate as valueless the bonds
that wed together Zeus and Hera;
and Aphrodite is by your account discarded with contempt,
the god who offers what's most close for humankind.
For man and wife the marriage bed, kept under guard
by justice, is more binding than an oath.
If they descend to murdering each other,

220   and you are to go easy, not applying your full fury,
then it's not right, I say, for you to drive Orestes out.
I find you're too concerned about one side,
and far too lenient with the other.
Athena shall arrange a trial to judge these issues.

CHORUS LEADER

Well, I shall never give up harrying that man.

APOLLO

Go on, pursue him; make more trouble for yourselves.

CHORUS LEADER

Don't you attempt to whittle down my rights.

APOLLO

I wouldn't want your rights, not even as a gift.

CHORUS LEADER

Because you stand secure beside the throne of Zeus:

230   but I am drawn on by a mother's blood,
and shall pursue this man until I have exacted justice.

[The Erinyes set off in pursuit of ORESTES.*]*

APOLLO

And I shall take care of my suppliant.
A suppliant's anger, if he is betrayed,
is fearsome for the gods as well as men.

[APOLLO *goes back into the temple, leaving the stage empty.*]

Scene 5

[*Athens: Enter* ORESTES, *exhausted, he upproaches the statue of* ATHENA.]

ORESTES

Mistress Athena, I have come here on the orders of Apollo:
please receive the wanderer with favor.
I am not seeking refuge with my hands polluted:
any stain has been long blunted and abraded
through my journeys and my time with other people.
240   I've traversed both rugged land and seas
in my obedience to Apollo's oracle;
and here I am before your temple and its image.
Here I stay, and wait for final judgment.

     [*Enter* CHORUS *in pursuit, like dogs on the track.*]

CHORUS LEADER

Aha! Clear traces of our man!
Run down the clues of the informant with no voice:
like hounds that track a wounded deer,
we're scenting out a trail of dripping blood.
My guts are gasping with our long, exhausting toils,
for we have scavenged every part of earth,
250   and skimmed across the seas, though with no wings.
And now at last . . . he's cowering somewhere here—
the whiff of human blood is smiling out at me.

CHORUS

        Search, search, and search again.
        Look all round for the man.
        Don't let the matricide
        escape with crime unpaid.
        Ah! Here he is!

His arms hold in embrace
the statue of the goddess.
260   He's hoping for legal trial,
but that's not possible.
A mother's pulsing blood
once spilled upon the ground
can't be fetched up again;
it soaks in and is gone.
In return you must give
your red liquor, while alive,
so that eagerly we gulp
from your veins the sour syrup.
Once we've drained you hollow,
we shall drag you down below.
There you'll see all who've sinned
270   against god or guest or kin.
For Hades keeps a tally
of every human folly,
and writes them down retained
in the ledger of his mind.

ORESTES

I've learned in my ordeals when is the time to speak
and when to keep my silence: at this crisis,
with a teacher's wise advice, I should now speak.
280   The blood upon my hands is fading, sleepy;
and pollution from the killing of my mother
has been washed away, purged by Apollo at his hearth.
And I could tell of many I have visited
while causing them no harm.
So now I speak with purity and call upon Athena,
mistress of this land, to come and bring me help.
That way she shall recruit myself, my country,
290   and the Argives as true allies for the rest of time.

So whether she's in Africa to help her friends,
beside the Triton's flow, where she was born,
or else surveying Phlegra's landscape, like a bold commander,
I now call on her to come—a god can hear far off—
so she may set me free.

CHORUS LEADER

No, not Apollo, not Athena can protect you
300　　from the fate of wandering disregarded,
ignorant of feeling glad—
a dinner for us goddesses,
till drained of blood, a shadow.

　　[ORESTES *does not respond.*]
No reply? Contempt for what I say?
You have been reared, I tell you,
as an offering for me,
and you shall feed me live—
no need for ritual slaughter.
So listen to this hymn
that works to bind you tight.

Choral Song

CHORUS LEADER

　　Come then, let us link together
　　in our chorus, now that we are
　　set on showing off our gruesome
　　music. Firstly, listen how we
310　　make allotments among humans
　　as we think is upright justice:
　　when a man is pure in actions,
　　there's no threat of anger from us,
　　and he lives his life undamaged;

but the sinner who attempts to
hide his violent deeds of murder—
we bear witness for the victim,
and extract the blood-price from him
so he pays the final reckoning.

CHORUS

Mother Night, my mother Night,
now hear me.
As a goddess of revenge
you bore me.
Yet Apollo's trying to
deprive me
of my rights by snatching off
this cringing,
consecrated creature from
my clutches,
which should be sacrificed
for bloodshed.
     Over our victim
     chant our refrain,
     Erinyes' hymn,
     driving insane,
     destroying his mind,
     binding his brain—
     tune without music,
     withering refrain.

Moira's thread has spun for us
this province:
to maintain forever as
our essence
power to follow with pursuit
untiring

those who've killed their closest kin
uncaring,
right down to the world below,
relentless.
Even there they are not free
340 entirely.

  Over our victim
  sing our refrain,
  Erinyes' hymn,
  driving insane,
  destroying his mind,
  binding his brain—
  chant without music,
  withering refrain.

This standing was allotted to us
(350) from our birth:
to share no common feasting with
the gods above;
we have no part in rituals that
don white robes.
Our chosen role is as destroyers
of a house
when violent strife leads one to killing
kin most close;
then we wear down his strength and drain
him to a husk.
Because we free the other gods from
(360) this grim task,
they do not have to bring such cases
to the test.
And Zeus excludes our blood-soaked party
from his feast.

—

Men seem high and mighty
underneath the sky,
but they shrink and dwindle
to indignity,
370   crushed beneath the pounding
dances of our fury.
Down from above
I leap and stamp,
full weight of my leg,
limb strong enough
even to trip
an athlete's step
with no escape.
Ignorant he tumbles,
damaged in his mind,
dark cloud of pollution
hovering around.
And over his household
380   grieving voices spread.

This is our task: resourceful we
make it complete and done;
long we remember wrongs, and press
implacably on men.
Away from gods we do our work
in murk that sees no sun.

390   What person feels no awe and dread
when hearing of our writ,
granted to us by the gods,
invariable, complete?
My state is honored, though beneath
the earth with no sun's light.

Scene 6

[*Enter* ATHENA.]

ATHENA

From far away I heard a cry for help—
I was at Troy, where I was marking out the share of land
400   allotted by the leaders of the Greeks to me,
for the Athenians to keep forever as a special gift.
I've hastened all the way from there,
though not with wings, my snake-cloak whirring in the wind.
And now I see this strange new gathering of visitors.
I feel no fear, but still I am astonished at the sight.
Who are you—all of you, I mean?
This stranger by my statue,
        [*To the Erinyes.*]
410   and you—you don't resemble
any gods known to the gods,
nor do you have a form like that of any humans.
But it would be wrong of me to speak
discourteously of those who've given no offense.

CHORUS LEADER

You shall hear everything concisely, child of Zeus.
We are the daughters born of Night;
and in the world beneath the earth
we're known as Curses.

ATHENA

So now I know your birth and title.

CHORUS LEADER

Next you should learn of our prerogatives:
(420)   we harry people-killers from their homes.

ATHENA

Where does the killer's running reach its end?

CHORUS LEADER
Some place where joy is quite unknown.

ATHENA
And that's the way you're hustling this man here?

CHORUS LEADER
We are: he thought it right to be his mother's killer.

ATHENA
With no compulsion? Or in dread of some fierce anger?

CHORUS LEADER
Could any be enough to spur a man to kill his mother?

ATHENA
(430)   There are two parties here, and I've heard only half.

CHORUS LEADER
Then test the case, and pass your judgment honestly.

ATHENA
And would you really hand to me the final outcome?

CHORUS LEADER
Indeed, if you respect us in return for our respect.

ATHENA [*To* ORESTES.]
Now, stranger, what have you to answer in your turn?
Tell me your country, family, and fortune;
and then defend yourself against their hostile charges—
440   if, that is, you are a solemn suppliant,
and taking this position by my statue out of trust in justice.

ORESTES
Athena, I shall first allay your anxious question.
I'm not here beside your image with my hands polluted.
I'll give a weighty proof of this: it is laid down
a man with blood upon his hands is not allowed to speak
450   until he has been cleansed by one with power to purify.
Well, I've been purged in other places,
both by sacrificial blood and by the flow of water.
So now I'll tell you of my family: I am from Argos,

son of Agamemnon, marshal of the naval force—
and you, with him, reduced Troy's city to a nothing-place.
And yet he died a squalid death when he came home.
My dark-intentioned mother slaughtered him
460 once she had cloaked him in a rich-embroidered net,
complicit with his murder in the bath.
And I, when I eventually returned from exile,
killed my mother—I do not deny it—
to make her pay the price for killing my dear father.
And Apollo shares responsibility for this,
since he proclaimed that I would suffer
heart-impaling agonies if I did nothing to the guilty ones.
Now it's for you to pass your judgment:
was it with injustice or with justice that I struck?
Whatever way you deal with me,
I shall assent to your decision.

ATHENA

470 This issue is too grave for any human
to assess decisively.
And it would not be right even for me
to pass a judgment which is bound to stir such anger.
On the one side, you've approached my temple
as a suppliant pure and free of harm:
these, on the other side, possess a function
that is far from airily dismissed.
And if they don't emerge victorious in this affair,
then they shall drizzle poison of resentment,
which, as it falls upon the ground,
will spread consuming plague.
480 That's how things stand—and either course
seems bound to bring down rancor.
So, since the issue has advanced this far,
I shall establish here a charter for all time:

a board of jurors, bound by solemn oath,
who shall be judges in the case of homicide.
    [*To both sides.*]
You therefore should assemble here your witnesses
and evidence supportive for your case.
Meanwhile, I shall select the finest of my citizens,
and gather them to pass conclusive judgment here.

                    [*Exit* ATHENA; ORESTES *stays.*]

Choral Song

CHORUS

490   If these new rules now overrule,
then unjust justice will prevail
to win the mother-killer's cause.
This act will set all humans loose
from decency; set people free
to murder with impunity;
leave parents helpless to stop harm
at children's hands in future time.

500   Unhindered by our manic gaze,
all kinds of death shall be released.
Though all about the victims claim
they have been harmed by kindred crime,
they will not find that there's redress
in answer to their anguished cries.
And though they try to stem their pain,
their remedies shall be in vain.

No use for anyone to shout
510   when they have been struck down:

"O Justice, O Erinyes
upon your lofty throne!"
Although a new-harmed father or
a mother's anguish calls
for pity, it's no use because
the house of Justice falls.

There is a way that terror can
improve the minds of men,
520   and fear prove beneficial since
good sense is reached through pain.
Those who do not cultivate
at heart a sense of fear—
the same for cities as for men—
will not hold Justice dear.

Don't praise a life oppressed,
nor yet a life dispersed
in careless anarchy.
In every sphere the god
530   empowers the middle way.
I frame a thought that's apt:
proud arrogance indeed
springs from impiety,
while from a mind with health
develops longed-for growth
of true prosperity.

I say that everyone
should treat the altar-stone
of Justice with respect;
540   don't kick it in contempt
for some imagined gain.

There will be punishment.
What's fixed remains secure:
with time it takes effect.
In view of this, be sure
to put first parents' care,
and treat guests with respect.

550   The man of unforced justice
will be securely prosperous:
the man of lawless daring—
pirate-fashion steering
a cargo overloaded
with goods unjustly looted—
will end with sail in tatters,
and with his mainmast shattered.

He cries out from the circles
of overwhelming whirlpools,
but there is none to hear him.
560   God mocks the man so certain
that he's immune from dangers.
He cannot ride the breakers;
wrecked on the reef of Justice,
he drowns unwept, unnoticed.

Scene 7

[ATHENA *reenters with jurors, who bring on benches and two voting urns. It emerges that the scene is now set on the hill of the Areopagus.*]

ATHENA

Now let the herald call the people here to order;
and let the piercing trumpet ring out loud and clear.

570 For as this council is assembled, silence is appropriate
     so that the city as a whole may listen to my charter.
     This will stand for all of future time,
(573) so justice may be well decided here.
(681) Now listen to my charter, citizens of Athens,
     you who are the judges in this trial,
     the first trial ever held for bloodshed.
     This just assembly shall hold good
     for my Athenians for evermore.
     It shall convene upon this outcrop,
     the encampment of the Amazons,
     when they invaded and then fortified
     this citadel confronting the Acropolis.
     And here they sacrificed to Ares, which is why
(690) this hilltop has been named the Areopagus.
     And here the sense of awe and inborn fear
     shall keep my citizens by day and night
     from doing wrong—provided they themselves
     do not revise and tamper with the laws.
     If you pollute clear water with bad effluent
     and dirt, you'll never find it good to drink.
     So I advise my citizens to venerate a way of life
     that's neither anarchy nor yet oppression either.
     And do not expel the element of fear
     entirely from the city—who can live a life
     that's just, with no deterrent fear at all?
(700) If you maintain this kind of just respect,
     you'll have protection for both land and city
     of a strength no other humans have achieved.
     So this assembly here—immune from love of gain,
     full of respect and fierce in righteous anger,
     wakeful over those who sleep—
     this I establish as a fortress for the land.
     I have dwelled long on this advice

(708)   for all my citizens for all of future time.
        ‹But now, before proceedings are begun,
        it is the proper time for witnesses
        to be assembled. Are there any here
        who wish to take their stand before our court?

            [*Enter* APOLLO.]

APOLLO

        Yes, queen Athena, I have come in haste,
        departing from my shrine at Delphi
        to be present here.

ATHENA

        It's only right, my lord Apollo, that you›
(574)   exercise your power in your own province.
        How is this issue of concern to you?

APOLLO

        I've come to act as witness for this man:
        he is my suppliant who looked for refuge at my hearth,
        and there I purified him after bloodshed.
        And I shall speak on his behalf,
580   since I am answerable for the killing of his mother.
        So begin proceedings, and conduct
        the case as you know best.

ATHENA

        I do hereby begin proceedings.

            [*To the Erinyes.*]

        It is for you to make your case,
        since it is proper for the prosecution to be first to speak,
        and to explain the issue from the start.

CHORUS LEADER

        We may be many, yet we shall each speak incisively.

            [*To* ORESTES.]

        And you must give your answers point by point.
        So this first: did you kill your mother?

ORESTES

I killed her, yes. There is no way I can deny the deed.

CHORUS MEMBER 1

Three falls are needed—that's already one!

ORESTES

590   You claim that, but I'm not yet on the floor.

CHORUS MEMBER 2

Then next you have to say: how did you murder her?

ORESTES

I say I drew my sword and slit her throat.

CHORUS MEMBER 3

And who persuaded you? Whose plan was this?

ORESTES

The oracle of this god here, as he's my witness.

CHORUS MEMBER 4

The prophet authorized your mother-killing?

ORESTES

Yes—and, thus far, I stand by what has happened.

CHORUS MEMBER 5

But when the vote entraps you, then you'll change your tune.

ORESTES

I keep on trusting. And my father helps me from the grave.

CHORUS MEMBER 6

You kill your mother, and then pin your faith on corpses!

ORESTES

600   I do, because she had been doubly stained.

CHORUS MEMBER 7

What do you mean? Explain this to the judges.

ORESTES

In murdering her husband, she destroyed my father too.

CHORUS MEMBER 8

But you are still alive: she's been absolved through death.

ORESTES

So, when she was alive, why did you not chase after her?

CHORUS MEMBER 9

She did not share his blood, the man she killed.

ORESTES

And do I share my mother's blood?

CHORUS LEADER

Of course you do. She nurtured you within her womb,
you loathsome murderer. Would you deny
your mother's blood, the nearest to your own?

ORESTES [*turning to* APOLLO]

610   Please stand, Apollo, as my witness now:
explain if I had justice on my side in killing her.
I can't deny I did it—that's a fact—
but give your judgment if my shedding of this blood
was justified or not.

APOLLO

Then I declare to you, who represent
this mighty charter set up by Athena:
it was justified.
I am a prophet and can never lie:
from my prophetic throne I've never said a thing,
concerning man or woman or a city,
not one word which was not authorized
by great Olympian Zeus.
I would advise you to appreciate
just how supreme this justice is,

620   and act in concert with the father's will—
there is no oath that binds more strongly than does Zeus.

CHORUS LEADER

So Zeus, by your account, conveyed to you this oracle,
which told Orestes to take vengeance for his father's death,
and to account his mother's claims as valueless?

APOLLO

Just so—because they're not to be compared.
This was the killing of a noble man,
distinguished by the scepter, gift of Zeus;
and, what is more, it was a woman laid him low—
yet nothing like the arrow of some warlike Amazon.
No, listen how it was, Athena,
630 and you jurors sitting here to give your votes.
When he had come back from the war,
where he had managed mostly well,
she welcomed him with lavish words;
and then, as he was lying in the bath,
she tented him inside a robe,
and, with him fettered in this crafty cloak of cloth,
she struck.
This is the sad tale of his death,
a man revered by all, commander of the fleet.
I emphasize this so the people gathered
to decide this case may feel the sting of it.

CHORUS LEADER

640 According to your version, then, you claim that Zeus accords
a father's death the heavier weight.
Yet he himself tied up his ancient father, Cronus.
Is not that a blatant contradiction?
I call upon you listeners to confirm this point.

APOLLO

You loathsome, god-detested monsters!
Zeus could loose mere chains—there is a mass of ways
of getting those unlocked, with no harm done—
but once the soil has gulped the life-blood of a man,
there is no way to stand him up again.
My father can reverse all other things
650 by turning them this way and that, without much effort,
but for this he has composed no counterspell.

CHORUS LEADER

Now think what your defense of this man means.
He's spilled his mother's blood upon the ground,
his own shared blood: how can he then
inhabit his ancestral home in Argos?
How could he stand by altars that are communal?
What brotherhood could have him at their rites?

APOLLO

I shall explain this; and you'll see that I am right.
The person who is called the mother
is no parent of the child, merely the feeder
of the new-implanted embryo.
660   The true begetter is the one who thrusts;
and she is like a stranger acting for a stranger:
she keeps the seedling safe, provided no god injures it.
I offer an exhibit that will prove the point
and show a father can give birth without a mother:
here stands the daughter of Olympian Zeus as witness.
She was never cultured in the darkness of a womb.
And I, Athena, shall so far as I am able
make your city and its people great.
I've guided this man to your hearth
670   so that he may stay loyal for all of future time,
and you may gain him and those after him as allies,
ever standing firm as pledges for the children of these men.

ATHENA

Now I instruct these jurors to apply
their honest judgment, and to cast their votes.
Enough has now been argued.

> [The jurors proceed to vote in the course of the following
> dialogue.]

CHORUS LEADER

Well, we have fired off all our arrows,
So we wait to see what way the issue is decided.

APOLLO

> You've heard what you have heard,
>
> 680   So, strangers, when you vote, revere your oath.

CHORUS MEMBER 1 [*to the jurors*]

(711)

> I would advise you not to underrate our claims:
>
> we could become a harmful presence for this land.

APOLLO

> I tell you to feel fearful of my oracles from Zeus,
>
> and not to leave them barren.

CHORUS MEMBER 2 [*to* APOLLO]

> If you embark on bloodshed—matters not your business,
>
> the temple of your oracle will not stay pure.

APOLLO

> Was Zeus then in the wrong when he assessed
>
> the case of Ixion, the world's first homicide?

CHORUS MEMBER 3

> Whatever you may say, if we don't win this case,
>
> 720   we shall stay on to be a menace for this land.

APOLLO

> You have no standing with the younger gods,
>
> nor with the older. I shall win.

CHORUS MEMBER 4

> You did this kind of thing back when you coaxed
>
> the Moirai to release Admetus from mortality.

APOLLO

> Was it not right to do a favor for that virtuous man,
>
> especially in his hour of need?

CHORUS MEMBER 5

> You upset age-old functions when you fooled
>
> those ancient goddesses with wine.

APOLLO

> Well, soon, when you have lost this case,
>
> you shall be spewing toxic bile—
>
> 730   although it cannot harm your enemies.

CHORUS MEMBER 6

A younger god, you try to trample over me, the old,
and so I'll stay to hear the outcome of this trial,
still undecided whether I should turn my anger on this city.

[*The jurors' voting is now complete.*]

ATHENA

It is my place to give my judgment last:
and I shall cast this vote in favor of Orestes.

[*She puts in her vote.*]

This is because no mother gave me birth,
and so in every way I'm for the male—
except for intercourse—with all my heart.
I'm strongly on the father's side,
and shall not grant a wife's fate precedence—

740   not one who killed her man, the master of her house.
It is the rule that, if the votes are equally divided,
the defendant wins.
And now, you jurors who've been trusted with this task,
be quick and tip the vote-stones from the urns.

[*The vote-tellers turn out the urns and count.*]

ORESTES

Phoebus Apollo, which way will this judgment go?

CHORUS LEADER

O mother Night, dark mother, do you see?

ORESTES

Now it is either hanging or the light of life for me.

CHORUS LEADER

For us it's nothingness or keeping our prerogatives.

CHORUS LEADER

Count up the emptied votes correctly, strangers.

ORESTES

Give justice your supreme respect as you decide.

CHORUS LEADER

750   A lapse of honesty can cause immeasurable harm.

ORESTES

A single vote can make or break a house.

ATHENA [*after being informed by the vote-tellers*]

This man has been acquitted of the charge of murder,
since the tally of the votes is equal for both sides.

[APOLLO *departs.*]

ORESTES

Athena, you have saved my heritage.
It's you who have restored me in my home
when I was dispossessed of fatherland.
And Greeks will say:
"This man is once again a man of Argos,
rich in his ancestral property.
He owes this to Athena and Apollo
and, third, all-achieving Zeus, the guardian."

760   Zeus gave my father's death his full respect,
and saved me from my mother's champions.
And now, as I head home, I swear an oath
to this whole country and its people,
good for all of future time:
no leader of my land shall ever marshal here
a hostile armored force.
If any should transgress this oath of mine,
then I myself, from in my tomb,
shall set against them fatal obstacles;

770   and make their march ill-omened and demoralized,
till they regret the undertaking.
But so long as they stay firm and true
toward this city of Athena with alliance in the field,
then I shall look on them with favor.
So farewell to you, and to the people

who maintain your city in their care.
May you hold fast a grip upon your enemies
that brings security and victory.

[*Exit* ORESTES.]

Scene 8

CHORUS

    You younger gods have ridden down
    the ancient laws,
    wrenching them roughly from my hands
    and into yours.
780   Deprived of rights, and full of rage,
    I'll blight this earth
    with poison, poison from my heart
    to pay back grief.
    I'll drip it on the soil to make
    foul cankers sprout,
    mildews that bring to children death
    and foliage blight—
    O Justice!—make plagues sweep the land
    and rot the soil,
    rot human flesh. What can I do?
    I mourn, I howl.
790   These citizens have made us fools,
    so we, dark Night's
    dear daughters, are consumed by grief,
    deprived of rights.

ATHENA

I must persuade you that you should not take offense
with such extreme resentment.
Understand: you were not beaten,

since the votes came out as truly equal,
and with no disgrace to you.
There was, though, clear-cut testament from Zeus,
delivered by the god who gave the oracle himself,
which said Orestes should not come to harm
because of what he'd done.
So you should not rain down
800   such deadly rancor on this land.
Hold back your anger; don't create a sterile desert
by exhaling poison droplets,
acid froth that eats at healthy seed.
I give my solemn promise: you shall have
a cavern-dwelling in this land, where you shall take
your seats on glistening stones beside your altars,
and receive due worship from these citizens.

CHORUS

You younger gods have ridden down
the ancient laws,
wrenching them roughly from my hands
and into yours.
810   Deprived of rights, and full of rage,
I'll blight this earth
with poison, poison from my heart
to pay back grief.
I'll drip it on the soil to make
foul cankers sprout,
mildews that bring to children death
and foliage blight—
O Justice!—make plagues scour the land
and rot the soil,
rot human flesh. What can I do?
I mourn, I howl.

820   These citizens have made us fools,
            so we, dark Night's
            dear daughters, are consumed by grief,
            deprived of rights.

ATHENA

You do still have your rights.
Do not be so incensed; and don't, as gods,
infect the land of humans with foul blight.
I too have my support—
I should not need to mention Zeus—
and I'm the only god who knows about the key
to where his thunderbolt is locked away.
But there's no call for that:
be open to persuasion by my words.
830   Don't hurl about these vitriolic threats
to poison every fruit that grows.
Soothe down the seething storm-waves of your rage,
so you may be most solemnly revered,
and stay as fellow settlers here.
When you are given first fruits from this fertile land,
receiving sacrifices to promote good childbirth
and good marriage, you shall be
forever grateful for this pledge of mine.

CHORUS

            For me to be demeaned,
            despite my age-old mind!
            To stay in this land where
            pollution's everywhere!
840   Such force is in my breath,
            its blast is full of wrath.
            Such pain is this that jabs
            me deep beneath my ribs.
            Hear me, my mother Night:

the gods' deceitfulness
has stripped me of old rights,
and made me nothingness.

ATHENA

I shall be patient with your anger,
seeing you are older and far wiser than I am—
850   though Zeus has granted me intelligence as well.
I tell you, if you part from here
in favor of some other people's land,
then you shall come to feel fierce longing for this place.
As time flows on, and as the standing
of these citizens grows great, you should possess
an honored dwelling near to their Acropolis,
where men and women would bring offerings far greater
(857)   than you would receive from any others.
(867)   This is the kind of future you may choose
to have from me: to do good deeds,
and to secure good treatment, and to share
good privileges in this land most favored by the gods.

CHORUS

870   For me to be demeaned,
despite my age-old mind!
To stay in this land where
pollution's everywhere!
Such force is in my breath,
its blast is full of wrath.
Such pain is this that jabs
me deep beneath my ribs.
Hear me, my mother Night:
the gods' deceitfulness
has stripped me of old rights,
880   and made me nothingness.

ATHENA

I shall untiringly remind you of these benefits,
to make quite sure you never will have cause
to say that you, more ancient gods, because of me,
the younger, and these human guardians of this city,
have been made to wander,
disrespected exiles from this place.
But if you give Persuasion her due reverence,
Persuasion who imparts enchantment to my words,
then you will stay.
And if you do not wish to stay,
it still would not be right for you to bear down
with your fury or bring harm upon these people,
890   seeing that there is a way for you to be a sharer
in this land, with privileges here forevermore.

CHORUS LEADER

Athena, queen, what is this place you tell me I shall have?

ATHENA

One that's secure from all distress. Accept it, do.

CHORUS LEADER

And if I did, what privileges would there be for me?

ATHENA

No house could thrive except with your support.

CHORUS LEADER

Will you yourself make sure I have such influence?

ATHENA

I shall, through favoring those who show you reverence.

CHORUS LEADER

And do you pledge me this for all of future time?

ATHENA

The things I say I'm bound to carry through.

CHORUS LEADER

900   You are enchanting me, I think—I'm shifting from my rage.

ATHENA

And once you're safely in this land, you shall gain friends.

CHORUS LEADER

What themes should I compose, then, for this place?

ATHENA

Such things as follow on a wholesome victory,
drawn from the earth and sea and air.
So sing to make the breezes blow
across a ground that is well warmed with sun;
and to ensure the produce of the earth and flocks
may yield abundantly, unfailing through the years,
to benefit these citizens;

(910)   and sing for human seed to issue in safe births.
For like a gardener, I take tender care
to cultivate the stock of these just men,
and wish to keep them free from grief.
Such matters are for you; and I shall make it sure
that on the field of war this city shall emerge
with victory conspicuous among mankind.

Scene 9

CHORUS

Yes, I am gladly accepting
Athena's offer of home;
and I'll not go rejecting
a city held in esteem
by mighty Zeus and by Ares
920   for its protection of shrines
prized by the gods of the Hellenes.

I conjure blessings to come:
livelihood swelling in plenty,
warmed by the rays of the sun.

ATHENA

I confer a favor on these
citizens by asking powerful
gods, not easily placated,
to inhabit here. The whole of
930   human being is their province;
and the man who draws their anger
can't tell where the lashes come from
as he is impelled to face them.
He may bluster, but a silent
doom destroys him through their anger.

CHORUS

I shall now tell of my blessings:
I pray no tree-blighting wind
940   or bud-searing blasts of the dog days
may trespass into this land,
nor any plague of the fruit crops
encroach. And may the god Pan
raise all the flocks impregnated
with double lambs. And may grain
grow from the earth in its richness,
refreshed by the god-given rain.

ATHENA

Listen to these pledges, guardian
950   citizens, what things they promise!
Great the power that they dispose of,
these Erinyes, both for the
dead below and things for humans.
Clearly they direct the shape of

lives of others: some they give a
world of music, while they make the
days of others blurred with weeping.

CHORUS

> I prohibit untimely death,
> mischance that lays men low;
> may all lovely young women claim
> a husband and a home.
> This I call for from you, Moirai,
> my mother's sister powers,
> gods who allocate what's right;
> you share in every house,
> charged with influence for all time,
> most honored in all ways.

ATHENA

> I'm delighted how they offer
> kindly goodwill to my country.
> And I'm glad Persuasion looked with
> favor on my language as I
> coaxed them from their harsh refusals.
> Zeus, the god of civic meeting,
> won the day. So now we're rivals
> in our giving out of blessings.

CHORUS

> And I pray that internal strife,
> a harm that never wanes,
> shall not ever unleash its scourge
> within the city's walls.
> May the dust never drink the blood
> of citizens as it's shed,

960

970

980

spur for retaliation
and slaughter making mad.
May they compensate joy for joy
as benefit is shared,
and agree on whom they oppose—
thus many ills are cured.

ATHENA

You see how they're tracing paths of
gracious wording. I can see how
blessings for my citizens will
990   come yet from these fearsome faces.
You should always treat these kind ones
kindly and respect them: that way
you shall keep your land and city
glorious in the ways of justice.

CHORUS

Go with joy, yes, go with joy,
wise in your prosperity,
go with joy, Athenians,
dear in your proximity
to the dearest child of Zeus.
1000   So in time you reach sound sense,
held high in the father's thoughts
and Athena's winged embrace.

[During the following speech, women of all ages, attendants
at ATHENA's temple, come onstage with flaming torches.]

ATHENA

Go with joy, you also! I shall
walk in front to show you to your
dwelling by the light of sacred
torches carried by this escort.
Once you're under earth, then ward off
all disaster from this country;
send instead the gain of victory.

[To the jurors.]
> And you who sustain the city,
1010 > it is time for you to lead on
> these new settlers. And show favor
> in return for generous favor.

CHORUS

> Go with joy, yes, go with joy,
> I repeat to all who hear,
> both divine and humans who
> hold Athena's city here.
> If you stay firm and reverence
> my new settling-place,
> you will not have any cause
1020 > to complain in all your days.

ATHENA

I'm grateful for these benedictions.
Now, illumined by the blaze of torches,
I shall come along with you
to your place down underneath the earth.
And you shall be attended by the women
who protect and serve my statue.
Yes, the flower of all the land of Athens
will escort you there, a splendid gathering
of girls and women, young and old.
> *[To the women.]*
It's right for you to pay them honor,
draping them around with purple robes.
Then let the flaring lights proceed,
1030 so that this kindly company may grant our land
for all of time a favorable fortune with fine men.
> *[The procession begins to move offstage, led by* ATHENA,
> *followed by the Erinyes with the attendant women, followed*
> *by the jurors.]*

SECONDARY CHORUS [*of women attendants*]
> Come now to your house,
> glorying in your powers,
> you daughters of dark Night,
> with kindly escort lit.
>> Lift up your joyful sound,
>> you people of this land!
> Down beneath the earth
> you shall have a wealth
> of praise and sacrifice
> in your primeval space.
>> Lift up your joyful call,
>> you people one and all!

1040
> With kindly theme
> for this land, come,
> you Solemn Gods;
> and take your joy
> in torches' flame,
> along your way.
>> Raise the triumph-cry!
>> Praise in harmony!
> Assured in peace,
> approach your house.
> All-seeing Zeus
> with Moira joins
> to bless Athena's
> citizens.
>> Raise the triumph-cry!
>> Praise in harmony!

[*The procession moves off.*]

NOTES

Please note that the line numbers are those of the Greek text, not of the translation.

Agamemnon

3   Agamemnon and his younger brother Menelaus are often paired as the "Atreidai," or "sons of Atreus." In the *Oresteia*, they rule jointly at Argos; in Homer's epics, Agamemnon has his palace at Mycenae, not far from Argos, while Menelaus rules at Sparta, quite far away to the south.

59   An *Erinys* (plural *Erinyes*) is usually translated as a "Fury"; but since the Erinyes are so important in the *Oresteia*, this translation retains their Greek identity. For further explanation of their role and centrality, see p. xxx.

116   Supposed to be the side of good omen.

123   Calchas was the seer and prophet who accompanied the expedition.

134   The virgin goddess Artemis traditionally protected wild animals.

168–75   A short stanza has been omitted here, because it is so obscurely allusive. Its subject seems to have been the violent acquisition of power, with reference to the succession passing from Uranus to Cronus to Zeus himself.

191   Aulis is a bay on the mainland coast just across the strait from the island of Euboea. There are strong, frequently reversing currents in this strait.

281   Clytemnestra starts from Hephaestus because he is the god of fire. For some of the places named, see the map on p. xi.

341   The Greeks did commit some notorious sacrilege when they sacked Troy.

419   "Aphrodite" here means Menelaus' desire for sex, because without Helen he is inconsolable.

438   Ares, the god of war, is evoked as a gold trader.

511   Scamander is the main local river at Troy.

513   Apollo had been opposed to the Greeks at Troy.

681ff. In Greek the syllables *hele-*, used as a prefix before words such as "ships," mean "destructive of."

696   Simois was one of the rivers near Troy.

827   The leap from the wooden horse to the ground was famous.

870   Geryon was a legendary giant-man with three upper bodies; he was killed by Heracles in the course of one of his labors.

881   Phocis, where the child Orestes has been sent, was the area of central Greece to the east of Mount Parnassus.

914   Leda was the mother of both Clytemnestra, whose father was Tyndareus, and Helen, who was fathered by Zeus.

958   The highly prized purple dye was produced by a process that extracted it from murex shellfish.

1040 The story was that Heracles was sold as a slave to the Lydian queen Omphale.

1080 Cassandra calls Apollo her *apollon*, her "destroyer" (this is reflected by "appalling").

1096 The first allusion to the story of Thyestes' being served the meat of his own children.

1143 The song of the nightingale was often linked to the story of Procne, who killed her son, Itys, and then lamented him constantly after her metamorphosis into the bird.

1160 Acheron was one of the rivers of the underworld.

1186ff. These lines take the form of a riddle, to which the answer— Erinyes—is finally supplied. The apparently fantastical picturing of the Erinyes as a "chorus" will in the third play become literal.

1192 The allusion is to Thyestes' adultery with Aerope, the wife of his brother Atreus.

1233 The snake with two heads is in Greek the *Amphisbaena;* the female monster Scylla (already in the *Odyssey*) was sometimes envisaged with dogs' teeth around her vagina.

1297 It was regarded as auspicious when an animal went to the sacrificial altar of its own accord.

1386 A third libation was conventionally made to Zeus *soter* ("saver"); Clytemnestra makes her macabre variation to "Zeus, saver of the dead," meaning Hades.

1439   This alludes to Chryseis, the slave concubine of Agamemnon at the start of the *Iliad*. The following lines about Cassandra are strikingly obscene.

1468ff.   "Daimon" is used for the Greek *daimon*. This word indicates some sort of unspecified deity, but in this passage it is repeatedly tied to the curse on the house and family. The dissimilar brothers Agamemnon and Menelaus married the sisters Clytemnestra and Helen, who are alike in being bold and dangerous.

1524   This may bring to mind the story that Agamemnon used the false pretext of fetching Iphigeneia to Aulis to marry Achilles.

1558   An allusion to the ferry of Charon, which transported the newly dead across the river Acheron.

1629   A weak jibe, characteristic of Aegisthus, about Orpheus' powers to lead with his music.

Women at the Graveside

1ff.   The sole manuscript preserving this play begins at line 10 and does not contain the twenty to thirty lines that must have come before that point. Some of those lines survive in other sources, but most of the passage is lost; this translation supplies between angled brackets (< . . . >) some guesses as to the kind of things that might have been there in the original.

1   Hermes was associated with messages, trickery, and passage to and from the underworld (the realm of Hades). So he is especially relevant to this play.

6   Inachus was an important river running through the plain of Argos.

248   It was believed that the female viper bit the male to death after copulation; the baby snakes then killed the mother by biting their way out from her womb. So this is an apposite analogy.

308   The name *Moirai* is conventionally translated as "Fates," but it is more meaningful to retain their Greek name—see p. xxx. They are a group of goddesses, closely associated with the Erinyes, whose role is to ensure that humans get what they deserve, especially in punishment for misdeeds.

423   The "beat" of their dirge is evoked through exotic Eastern terms: "Arian" and "Kissian" both refer to parts of what is now Iran (formerly Persia). This suggests that the music and choreography of the chorus convey traces of the lands of origin.

439   This refers to the primitive ritual of *maschalismos*, in which the ears, nose, and genitals of dead men were cut off and put under their armpits in order to counteract the power of vengeance.

602ff.   This song accumulates mythical examples of destructive female passion to compare with Clytemnestra. The first is Althaea, who had been told of a log that would keep her son Meleager alive for as long as it smoldered. When he grew up and killed her brothers, she burned it.

613ff.   Scylla's father, Nisus, was the king of Megara. When the city was besieged by the Cretans, she was bribed by the offer of a gold necklace to cut off the magic lock of hair that kept her father strong.

631ff.   The women of the island of Lemnos killed all their husbands; they then paired up with the visiting Argonauts.

653ff.   The scene, which has previously been set at Agamemnon's tomb, is now "refocused" in front of the palace.

783ff.   Unfortunately, the manuscript version of this choral song contains many problems of text and interpretation, and quite a lot has been trimmed.

899   Here, the only time Orestes hesitates (and the first time he says "mother"), he turns to Pylades, who utters his first and only lines. Since Pylades comes from near Delphi, it is appropriate that he should speak for Apollo.

924   This apparently figurative expression for her revenge turns into the actual gathering of the Erinyes, as Orestes will see clearly at lines 1053–54.

935ff.   The manuscript of this song also contains many problems of text and interpretation and has been substantially trimmed.

1038ff. Suppliants who threw themselves on the mercy of a god would usually hold a branch of olive or laurel bound round with ribbons of wool. Apollo's famous shrine at Delphi contained a stone, the *omphalos*, which was held to be the navel of the earth; there was also a sacred fire that never went out.

1048   This epilogue by the Chorus plays a subtle variation on the trilogy structure of the plays. The third episode reflects the shape of this, the second play: what had seemed like a final resolution ("kind of savior") has turned out to be leading to yet further tribulations ("more a death knell"). The play ends with an unresolved question: What will happen in the fourth episode, viz the third play?

Orestes at Athens

2   Gaia ("Earth") and Themis ("Order," "Right") were traditionally said to have been the first gods worshipped at Delphi. The usual story of what happened next told about the dragon Pytho and its

violent defeat by Apollo; this is replaced here by what is emphasized as a peaceable succession.

9   Delos is the island in the Aegean Sea where Apollo and Artemis were born.

21   The temple of Athena *Pronaia* was below the main sanctuary to the southeast; it was on the road up from the gulf far below.

22   The large, numinous Corycian Cave is higher up, not far below the highest parts of Parnassus.

24ff.   Dionysus was believed to inhabit Delphi in the winter, while Apollo was away. The myth of how he punished his nephew Pentheus, the king of Thebes, was well known, although it was usually, as in Euripides' *Bacchae*, located on Mount Cithaeron rather than Parnassus.

27   The river Pleistus flows in the valley far below Delphi.

29   The priestess sat on a throne, or in other accounts on a tripod, and then the oracles were delivered through her voice.

40   The *omphalos* stone was oval-shaped and stood about a meter high.

50   Phineus was a mythical king who was pestered by the winged Harpies. The Gorgons were characterized by their horribly ugly faces and snaky hair.

140ff.   The original staging is uncertain. The opening lines of the Chorus were probably broken up between individual members.

234ff.   At this juncture, the setting of the play changes from Delphi to Athens, and a considerable amount of time is understood to have passed, with Orestes on the run and the Erinyes close on his heels. This brings out how long and relentless the pursuit has been.

292ff.   The significance of these two locations—the river Triton in Libya and Phlegra in Thrace—is not clear, except that they represent the distant south and north, respectively.

333   For Moira (plural Moirai), see p. xxx.

470ff.   It takes Athena's wisdom to see that while humans cannot solve this crisis by themselves, it cannot be resolved simply by divine will, either, since it has such human consequences. Her solution is to set up a jury under her supervision.

After 573   There is a major change here from the usual text as it is transmitted in the Greek manuscripts, as is indicated by the marginal line numbers. Athena's founding speech for the court (lines 681–708) has been moved back from some one hundred lines later to this context, where it makes appreciably better sense.

Before 574   A few lines have been added at the end of Athena's speech to make the arrival of Apollo less abrupt.

685 The Amazons were believed to be a tribe of warrior women, located in Thrace or in Asia Minor, who participated in various mythical conflicts. The usual myth was that they invaded Athens in reprisal for a raid mounted against them by Theseus.

641 The tradition was that when Zeus overthrew his father, Cronus, along with Cronus' Titan brothers, he imprisoned them below in Tartarus.

657ff. There is some evidence that this embryological theory had been put forward by some protoscientists around the time of Aeschylus. It can hardly be treated as definitive, however, since, for the whole trilogy so far, it has been taken for granted that the mother is indeed one of the two parents. Apollo's case is also diminished by his crude language in the next line.

676–80 and 711ff. During this dialogue the jurors come forward, one for each couplet, and deposit their votes. There were two urns, and the procedure was that each juror would put his hands into the top of both but drop the voting pebble into only one.

718 The mythical hero Ixion killed his father-in-law and so became the first murderer; he then appealed to Zeus for absolution and became the first suppliant.

723 In gratitude for hospitable treatment, Apollo arranged for Admetus, a king in Thessaly, to be spared from imminent death, provided someone else died for him (this is the story in Euripides' *Alcestis*). Apollo did this by getting the Moirai drunk.

734 In classical Athens, if the votes were tied, it was taken as acquittal, thanks to "the vote of Athena." Athena makes this declaration after the voting is over, and so does not influence the jurors with it. Her reasons are personal and supernatural; she does not offer her birth as a relevant consideration, as Apollo had done earlier.

858–66 Nine strange lines that clearly do not belong in this place have been omitted.

944 Pan was a god of the wilds, but he was also a patron of shepherds and their wandering flocks.

1028 These purple robes, which are put over the Erinyes' black ones, may allude to the robes worn by noncitizen settlers (metics) at the annual Panathenaia festival in Athens.

1043 and 1047 The call here is to raise the *ololygmos,* the "triumph-cry," which was especially associated with women. This has had sinister uses earlier in the trilogy, especially in connection with Clytemnestra, but is now used joyfully.

RECOMMENDED PRONUNCIATIONS OF PROPER NAMES

A verse translation necessarily has to incorporate some assumptions about the pronunciation of names and, especially, which syllable is to carry the most stress. The list below gives a rough phonetic transcription of the pronunciations adopted for the most recurrent names in this translation, with the stressed syllable in bold. Please note that these do not pretend to be the ancient Greek pronunciations, which in many cases were substantially different.

Aegisthus	Ee-**giss**-thuhss
Agamemnon	Agguh-**mem**-non
Apollo	Uh-**poll**-lo
Ares	**Air**-eez
Argive	**Are**-guyve
Argos	**Are**-goss
Artemis	**Art**-amiss
Athena	Uh-**theen**-uh
Atreus	**At**-trooss
Aulis	**Owl**-liss
Cassandra	Kass-**sand**-ruh

Clytemnestra	Clite-uhm-**nest**-ruh
Daimon	**Dye**-mon
Delphi	**Dell**-fee
Electra	Ell-**leck**-truh
Erinyes (plural)	E-**reen**-new-ezz
Erinys (singular)	E-**reen**-noose
Hades	**Hade**-eez
Hermes	**Herm**-eez
Iphigeneia	Iffy-jen-**nigh**-yuh
Menelaus	Mennuh-**lay**-uhss
Moira	**Moy**-ruh
Orestes	Aw-**rest**-eez
Priam	**Pry**-uhm
Pylades	**Pill**-uh-deez
Pythia	**Pithy**-yuh
Scamander	Scam-**mand**-uh
Thyestes	Thigh-**est**-eez
Zeus	**Zyouss**

ACKNOWLEDGMENTS

I am especially indebted to Josh Billings, my coeditor for the Norton Critical Edition, who offered much sage advice and encouragement (and even remarked on one passage as "like Emily Dickinson"!). Claire Catenaccio and Arabella Currie also made many helpful observations on the draft version. At Norton, Carol Bemis has been a great champion, and I am also grateful to Marie Pantojan, Rachel Goodman, Bonnie Thompson, and Harry Haskell for their various roles in producing the volume. At home, above all, I have to thank Beaty, as ever, for her love and support, Charis for keeping me alert, and Phoebe and Nat for keeping in touch.